UNSEEN

K.C. POITRAS

This book is for you, Eric. You continue to inspire me, support me and answer all my silly questions. Without you, none of my dreams of becoming a writer would not have become more than a dream.
I love you

I would like to dedicate this book to our kids. Skylar, Macy, Eden, Joshua, Christopher and Alyssa. May you always feel you hold a special place in our hearts, whether far or near. May you never feel unseen or lost, but always loved. You all are the reason we grow each day and learn. We will always be here with our door and arms open, waiting to see each of your smiles, triumphs, tears and life's hiccups.

DISCLAIMER:
During the time period this book takes place, punishment was severe in many ways. There are some graphic scenes that include what's called child abuse today.

ONE

STACY WAS TWO YEARS OLD.

George Robert's has had enough of the drinking and lack of care his wife, Victoria, gives to the kids. Uncertain what to do about all the arguing, he knew he had to leave her. He was at the end of his rope and could not take any more. Born in New Zealand, he had married her when she visited there. It was love at first sight. They had met one evening while he was on holiday. When Victoria headed back to the states, George followed her and made her his wife. It was only a matter of years before George discovered America was not what he had expected, nor was his marriage. Now raising four children the age of ten and younger, he yearned for his country and family and New Zealand. With little to no help from Victoria regarding the kids, he gave up. In New Zealand, George worked as a project engineer before he'd left, a sought after one at that. Everyone wanted him on their projects. He was a robust gentleman with deep brown eyes and a sharp jawline. His smile would melt the hearts of many women. Today, Victoria had plans with the neighborhood housewives. They had decided on a girl's day out.

Victoria was outside waiting for her friends to arrive. The dress she wore swished in the wind. She stood at attention like she was in the military, taking orders. Her chest heaved as she inhaled the salty morning air. *I could use a drink*, she thought. She continued to pace back and forth, feeling the warm sand tickle her feet. Impatiently, she waited for her friends. Spying them a block away, she raised her hand and waved at the group of women. Victoria remembered all she had learned from them. They had been friends for over fifteen years. She loved hanging out with them more than anything. She loathed having to raise kids; she wanted her single life back. Recalling the argument, her and George had last evening, she shivered. She'd admit she had been a little drunk.

"George, the damn kids are fine!" she had said when he seen them dirty and hungry. He'd just returned from work and now he had to attend to them.

"Victoria, you're drunk!" George exclaimed. As she slurred her words, she stumbles to their bedroom.

"I'm not drunkkk, ur an asshole." Victoria said as she stumbles to the bed and falls face down fully clothed.

Upon entering their bedroom George takes off her shoes and swings her legs onto the bed and covered her up. Shaking his head, with brows furrowed the anger on his face was clear as it grew red.

"Hi lady's let's get this party started, "Victoria shaking the memory from her head as she headed towards the group. Her senses sharp, with only one thing on her mind *a drink*. They had decided to go to the *Beach Box Café*, it was a quant restaurant, in Naples. The café right on the beach offered up drinks and food. Like most beach bars, it had outdoor seating and open-air facility with décor of a vacation oasis. The roar of the vacationers sounded deafening to their ears. Native Floridians hated tourist season, however appreciated the revenue they brought with them. They observed each other, trying to decide where to sit. Finally, Marisa broke the silence, grabbed Victoria's hand,

"Let's get this table outside. We prefer outdoors anyway and it's less crowed," her friend said as she pulled Victoria along. Their other friends followed them with drinks. Victoria admitted she did not want to fight with him anymore or raise four kids on her own. The group eyed each other skeptically. They all recognized Victoria had a drinking problem, which affected her ability to do for her young children. *She probably should have never married,* Victoria thought. Her husband, George Roberts, was no longer patient with her. However, he worked two jobs and attended school in hopes of having his own business.

He was a healthy man, with dark hair and a muscular frame. Respected in his country by everyone. She remembers when they were in New Zealand *how when George walked into an establishment, someone usually recognized him.* Shrugging off this nonsense of a mood, Victoria takes a long swig of her frozen daiquiri. As it trickled down her throat, she could feel its coolness. She always started slow when she drank. On the slim chance when Victoria wasn't drunk, she still didn't watch the kids closely enough. George was forever cleaning up her messes. The memory of last night's fight was still nagging Victoria.

"Victoria, you need to get help. Your drinking is out of control. You ignore the kids to the point of neglect." George said.

"Go to hell." Victory said in a huff. The neighborhood wives were filling her in on their upcoming plans for trips and nights out. Most of them with children were of the age they could stay alone.

"Earth to Victoria," one of her friends said. Laughing, Victoria held up her glass as she allowed all thoughts of the night before to leave her memory.

"Cheers." They all held up their cups and clanked them together for the first shot of the day. Tequila

"I'll leave tomorrow while Victoria is with her friends." George had told his buddies at work the prior day. It disappointed them they'd be losing an employee and a friend. However, he had confided in his boss and his boss supported and understood George must go. As the girls partied and laid on the beach, typical rich natives to Naples. A little too loud, on the verge of being drunk, they swam, listened to music and danced around. A few observers joined them in the festivities. Although all the ladies polished, they didn't come close to Victoria's beauty. Her skin, the color of the finest cream, and her hair shone in the sun. She knew she wanted and had planned to get it, as she eyed a cute gentleman who was visiting from California. It wasn't the first time she'd hooked up with someone.

Meanwhile, Brad would pick up Elsie and Robby, two of their kids. Brad was their uncle; they'd be better off staying behind with Victoria. He planned on taking their other two, both too small to fend for themselves. Stacy was only two years old, while Donald was four. He knew she couldn't raise them in her current condition. Stacy had the curliest locks of hair and the bluest eyes anyone had ever seen. His smile lit up any room and was contagious. He was a happy baby; he looked like a true *Gerber* baby. No, he couldn't leave him behind; he'd never survive his mom at this point. George thought Elsie, his daughter, a lanky ten-year-old with smooth blonde hair, took after her mom. George felt obligated to leave her. He knew she could help with cooking and cleaning for the boys, when their mom was out running around.

"Okay, where do you think you're off to?" Lindsey interrupted Victoria, who was hanging all over this young man.

"We're just going for a walk silly. We'll behave and be right back."

"Of course, honey. Be safe and behave!" Lindsey responded. She knew Victoria was full of shit. She will once again cheat, but oh well, that's her life, or at least that's what it had become. With a puzzled look on their faces, the ladies noticed Victoria had come back to join them without her new male friend. She shrugged them off with a wink and lifted her shoulders as to say, eh it's all good. With a short, uncertain smile towards Victoria, two of the ladies and Lindsey grabbed drinks and danced along to the music. Meanwhile, Victoria and Katrina took care of preparing lunch. Today they were keeping it simple: They had packed, crackers, smoked salmon and an assortment of cheeses.

After lunch the ladies decided to chill on their beach chairs and watch the sun set.

"Come eat, "George called out to the kids. They sounded like a herd of elephants as they ran through the house. Excited to have lunch together with him. This was rare due to his work schedule. While the children laughed and ate, George decided to have a scotch on the rocks. All his plans had been set and he'd be leaving soon enough, knowing Victoria wouldn't be home for hours if at all that night. After lunch George put the kids down for their naps. This gave him time to order a car to take them to the airport. Brad was picking the older two up in an hour.

Lindsey, Victoria's closest friend, was the last to leave the beach with her.

"So, are you sure? Victoria smiled, but her eyes looked glazed over. Maybe it was the

alcohol, or maybe the sheer joy of leaving with the gentleman friend.

"Yes, I'm sure. Have you seen him? He's hot." Victoria could hear the waves crash the

shoreline and she anticipated and evening with the guy on her arm. The sun had set, and there was a strange feeling, like nothing Victoria had ever felt.

She knew once she took that irrevocable step, there's would be no turning back. Shivering, although it was not cold, she took the strangers hands and walked with him down the beach. Turning to Lindsey, never looking more beautiful, Victoria said,

"I'll catch up with you tomorrow," as they hugged.

"I'll be waiting for details."

Both ladies knew this wouldn't be the case. Victoria never spoke of her indiscretions. Marisa headed off to her vehicle for a short drive home.

It was a brutal start of summer in Florida, and the heat felt like it could fry an egg. George wondered what time Victoria would show up that evening. He bathed Stacy and helped him get dressed. Suddenly, he heard Robby yell.

"Stop it! It's my turn."

George took a deep breath "boys knock it off," he yelled up the stairs.

In unison, Robby and Donald yelled, "Dad, tell him to leave me alone," at wits' end, George walked up the steps to assess exactly what was happening. About that time, Brad came in. He looked around, eyeing a pot boiling on the stove and Stacy sitting on the floor playing. He smiled, then the joy drained from his face as he heard the commotion upstairs.

"Boys, settle down, or I'll be up there to settle you down," he yelled, and they quieted down immediately. Loving their uncle, they ran down the stairs.

"Are you guys ready to go to my house and jump in the pool?" Brad said.

"Yes, yes," they jumped with joy as they retrieved the overnight bag George had put together for them. When Brad, Elsie and Robby had left, George sat to take a break, happy the other two were still napping. George let thoughts of the past flood through.

George returned to the kitchen as he said over his shoulder in a caustic undertone that was as sharp as a knife. "Victoria, you could help every once in a while."

"Good Evening to you too. I'm tired; I worked hard today."

Looking over at Victoria, George thought, how hard is drinking, is that her work. He shook his head. But it didn't matter. "Well, I've worked all day too."

As the tension built and they exchanged words, Victoria threw her hands up in the air. "I've got to tend to some things out back." slamming the door hard enough to jar the windows as she walked out. George fed the kids and put them down for the night. He wandered around the house and knew she'd be out late drinking. He cleaned up the afternoon mess and put the leftover food from dinner away. All the memories overtaking him and the thoughts of leaving in a few scant hours for the airport were overwhelming. He recalls one of their last fights, the one that made him realize it was over.

"Victoria, I don't know what you expect from me. I work and provide; that's what men do."

Victoria shot him a look that only a scorned man could describe and stood up. "Sleep on the couch. I'm going to bed." George rubbed his head and thought, shit, at least it's warm in here. He laid down on the couch and closed his eyes. Tired to the bone, George fell asleep within minutes.

Their second born Robby went over to the bed where Stacy was asleep, he covered him up and wondered how he didn't wake up during all the yelling. He was a blond-haired, blue-eyed kid like Stacy. He was a sweet boy and always looked out for Stacy. Robby was seven years old and had listened to his parents fight for too many years now. He got a paper route just to escape. He stashed his money in a shoebox in the attic for safekeeping. Even at seven, he was small and quiet as a snake, which made it easy for him to go up to the attic and play or count his savings. Although he should have been asleep. It was a creepy attic, with cobwebs everywhere. But he's a man, he told himself, and men aren't afraid of cobwebs or spiders, just mean old ladies. Once upstairs in the attic, Robby turned on the overhead light and quietly started playing with some of his little action figures. He ended up falling asleep on the floor in the attic

Donald, the third born, took after their father, as did Elsie. Both with blonde hair, heavier build, tall and awkward. Donald is four years old but seemed a little slow. He rocked himself to sleep and sometimes woke up finding he'd wet the bed. When this happened, he would hurry and clean up before anyone found out. His mother always knew when he did this because his bed was wet. All four children were vastly different, like mismatched sets of dishes.

As the last of the sun disappeared George woke up, he must have dozed off. The nightmares that always held his unconscious mind flooded his dreams as usual. He felt stiff, irritated, and wondered if would be any better. He got his shower, shaved, packed snacks for him and looked out the window for their car to arrive. Victoria had not returned home yet; he was relieved. He heard Elsie and Robby quietly playing upstairs. He knew he had a lot to do before the driver arrived.

"Hey, you two, we're leaving in about fifteen minutes," George said

"Ok dad. We're almost ready." Elsie said

He couldn't help but wonder what it would be like back in New Zealand. Could he rekindle his engineering career, he hoped so? Once the snacks were packed and loaded. George feared this was going to be a long journey across the country. His mood was somber; he didn't make this decision to leave lightly. Knowing it was the best decision for him, he suddenly realized he'd been holding her breath. He let out a deep exhale and took a few deep breaths. His chest was tight. It felt like a heavy weight pressing on him, he thought it must be anxiety and nerves. "Well, I have to write the letter to Victoria. Then we'll leave." George said out loud to the empty room. He grabbed a pen and paper as he sat at the kitchen table.

Dear Victoria,

It is with a heavy heart that I write to you. By the time you read this, I will be halfway around the world. I hope you will someday forgive me, but I cannot take it anymore. I miss my family. I'm lonely, and you and I haven't been civil for quite some time now. Brad has Elsie and Robby. You know how much they like visiting him. Donald and Stacy are going with me. I'm taking them to New Zealand, I must go; I know you won't understand. I hope you find what you're looking for, and Victoria, please get help with your drinking.

Goodbye Victoria

Letter wrote, he put it in an envelope and propped it up on the table. She would see it there where he usually left her mail each day. George took another look around. Suitcases packed and at the front door, he awaited the car. It was a scorcher of an evening with not a breeze to be had. As he looked through the window, he smiled and thought, well, at least he'd enjoy the weather back home. He hurried up to the attic where he found Donald playing, all sprawled out. He looked so small and fragile; he thought. George quickly grabbed the passports he had received a few weeks earlier, then said, "Donald, gather your toys, let's pack some up and get downstairs."

A sleepy Donald rolled onto his hands and knees, then got to his feet, rubbing the sleep from his eyes. He grabbed the few toys he wanted and went downstairs. He had only been awake from his naps a few moments prior to his dad finding him in the attic. George made himself a cup of coffee, knowing it would be a long night.

"It's time to go, Donald," George told them. He looked over at Stacy, picked him up, and gave him a toy to play with. The car showed up promptly and was now waiting for them. While George opened the door, Elsie and Donald buckled up in the back seat. The well-manicured young driver helped load the luggage, then returned to the driver's seat.

"Dad, where are we going?" Donald asked.

Thinking on his feet because this is one area he had forgotten to cover his bases in, he replied. "You know Robby and Elsie are visiting Uncle Brad. We'll I thought I'd take you and Stacy on some errands with me." Satisfied and forgetting the luggage, he accepted that answer and settled in for the ride.

"Dad, why do we get to go with you and not the others?" Donald said.

He turned to look at him. "Because they like to visit Uncle Brad and it's easier for me to only run errands with two of you guys instead of four. The two of you go there all the time to hang out with him."

Donald jabbed Stacy in his side. Stacy started to cry. "He poked me," With a no-nonsense look, George turned to look at them. He made it clear this would be the last time. "Stop it. Both of you. Donald, you know Stacy is smaller than you, don't be mean to your brother." Feeling scolded, Donald blushed and became quiet. Stacy, turned to look out the window, rubbing the spot he'd just been jabbed. They arrived at the airport, escaping little Stacy what was going on. However, Donald was a bit confused

"Hey sluggers, ready for an airplane ride?" He said to them. Both boys were excited and Started to run off from him.

"Hey, both of you get back over here now and help with the luggage. You must stay with me there are a lot of people here. You could get lost." Donald grabbed Stacy's hand and they returned to where their father waited.

"Where are we going dad? Donald asked.

"Home. We're going to New Zealand." Still puzzled, Donald accepted the answer for now. George figured out quickly he had more questions about their trip home.

They had arrived safely at South West Florida International and boarded their plane.

Having three stops, their first stop would be JFK for a nine-hour layover. George had already secured a hotel room for them while there. Not knowing much about the city, he figured they'd order room service, stay in and sleep until their next flight. Their next stop would be Singapore Changi Airport for a three-hour layover, where they would stay in the airport. Their third and final stop would be another overnight at Auckland Airport. Again, George had secured a hotel room at the airport for them. After completing their last leg of their journey of approximately 54 hours of travel over four long days they would land at New Plymouth Airport their destination. The trip took a toll on the kids as well as George. All in all, Donald helped entertain Stacy. He played with him while their dad slept. He kept him entertained, fed him, and then rocked him to sleep. Donald wandered around the plane and talked with other travelers.

"We're going to New Zealand to live," he told a passenger a few rows over.

"That's wonderful," said the passenger. He looked back a few rows and decided he should return to his seat. The flight had become a little bumpy. Alarmed he went to wake up his dad, gently shaking his arm.

"Dad, why is the flight so bumpy?"

At first, George had a hard time understanding what he meant, then he realized, and he laughed for the first time since leaving Naples.

"Donald, that's just turbulence it happens occasionally depending on weather and other things, it's ok." He comforts his son. Finally, Donald gives in to exhaustion and fell asleep. This left George to tend to Stacy. They would arrive in New Zealand the next day. George couldn't remember the last time he felt so bone tired. His eyes had bags under them, his shoulders slummed and his step less confident. All three of them were happy to have reached their destination and departed the plane. George's family met them at the airport. Collected their luggage and drove the few miles to their home in New Plymouth. It was a sight that George took in, and he felt an overwhelming sense of peace. As he looked around viewing some of the best surfing water and the mountains behind him. He sighed in relief and absorbed the beauty he remembered. Thrilled to be home with his family, and he couldn't wait to see his friends. They adored the baby and were excited to have their son home, and they hadn't even met their two grandchildren until now. Stacy was magical in their eyes. The sweet boy accepted hugs and kisses from these strangers. They enrolled the boys in school and taught them to swim and surf. While enrolled in preschool, Stacy would excel and adapt to his new surroundings. He became shy and clung to his dad. Donald adjusted to life there easily, and when not doing schoolwork, he played with little Stacy. George landed the engineering job of his dreams, and his career had taken off fast. They lived a busy life, and all appeared to be happy and adapting.

SEVERAL DAYS EARLIER...

Victoria walked into the house after she parked the car. She noticed there were no lights on anywhere. When she entered, she turned on the living room light. Growing more curious about where everyone was. She yelled out for George, listened, with no response. She shook her head and took off her sweater. She looked around, spotting the mail on the table and an envelope with her name on it. Curious, she opened the letter and read it. Then sat down on her favorite chair and hung her head in his hands. Victoria looked like a fish out of water with its guts cut out. The pain wrenched through her body as if it had cut her open. She knew they had problems. What she didn't expect was for him to take two of their kids and fly out of the country. She finally let go of the tears. Holding nothing back, she felt as empty as their house and as alone as the sun rose. She wept until there were no tears left to shed. What felt like days was only a few hours.

Later that day, she called her brother. She reported the news to him and asked if he could watch the boys tomorrow. She would be over after looking for a job. "Sure, Vic, you know they're always welcome. I'm sorry to hear about George. What a terrible thing for him to do. Is there anything you need?" Her brother said.

"No, I'm good. I'll see you tomorrow." With a long shaggy sigh, she hung up the phone and laid down in the middle of the floor where Stacy's baby blanket was. It was soft and smelled like her youngest son, which brought back the tears. Victoria felt like her heart was being ripped out all over again. Hungover, she fell asleep thinking she would never wash that blanket until Stacy returned.

TWO

STACY WAS NOW FOUR YEARS OLD AND STARTING KINDERGARTEN.

His vocabulary had grown as much as he had but, he had been having nightmares or seen a ghost, no one was sure which. As was usual, Stacy called out for his brother, "Donald, Donald." He found him with his head on the desk. He had fallen asleep while doing homework.

He ran downstairs, crying. Stacy had interrupted George for the third time this week.

"I want my aunt, dad."

George looked even more frustrated this time when he looked at him. "Stacy, it was only a dream. Calm down. Your aunt is not here; she's in America." A visibly shaken and upset Stacy returned to his room. Having trouble falling asleep, he screamed. No one could tell exactly what he said. It was very clear something troubled him. George suddenly knew what he had to do. The next morning after he rose and had a cup of tea, with much tribulation, He had to place an unpleasant call back to the states.

When the line connected, a man's voice said, "Hello, Haas residence. How can I help you?" Flabbergasted a man had answered the phone, it threw George off his game. He realized they'd received their final divorce over a year ago. He had no ties to the states or his ex-wife. Still, a trace of jealousy fluttered over him like a vast wave that unexpectedly knocked you down when you emerged into the ocean.

"Um, yes, is Victoria Roberts in?" He finally inquired.

The man's voice on the other end sounded sophisticated. His words pronounced with emphasis and masculinity. "No, she's out. May I tell her who is calling?" Albert said, Victoria's new man, contemplated if the gentleman on the other end had hung up.

"Can you have her call her ex-husband? she has the number. We need to speak about Stacy." George explained. Then hung up the phone. Albert was put out by the burst of information and the abrupt ending to the call. He tried to find his composure. Albert did not like any surprises, nor rudeness.

Meanwhile, in New Zealand, George wore a hat and a pair of sunglasses, the sun was shining bright. He and Stacy caught a lift to the airport. Little Stacy was being dragged along while his little legs tried keeping up. He didn't look around or slow down. Once Stacy was handed off to the stewardess, George spun around as if he was a tornado gaining speed and fled the scene; not turning to look back one time. Relieved that he was out of the airport, he lit a cigarette and was shuffled into the waiting car by the driver who held his door open.

The more Albert played back the conversation, the more upset he became. He is, after all, a New Yorker. This type of behavior was completely unorthodox. Although he and Victoria were unwed for now, he still stood at the head of the house and ran a tight ship. There was no room for nonsense among those that lived there. He was the ruler. He always believed in the pecking order and proper conduct. Robby and Elsie had learned the rules of the house swiftly. He had heaps of rules and consequences for every broken rule. He ran a military style tight ship, especially with kids that were not even his own. After hanging up the phone, he began to pace. While looking around, he questioned if he should go out and find Victoria or call her. Albert decided to wait until Victoria got home that afternoon. Thinking *nothing could be that important to interrupt her day out.* He tied his sandy blond hair back away from his face. Even from New York, Albert quickly adopted the beach boy vibes of an older area on the outskirts of Naples. He tied an apron behind his back, looked around the kitchen in preparation for dinner. His annoyance in the interruption showed in his body language. It was Saturday his day to cook.

He set pots down with a thud, abusing them. Summoned Robby and Elsie to get in there and help set the table. Robby reached the kitchen first, and he could tell Albert was angry. He reached for the dishes.

"Everything okay? When will mom be home?" Albert continued to chop the onions as if they were live spiders.

"No, mind your manners and get the table set." Robby and Elsie set the table.

A half an hour later, Victoria walked in, smiled at the boys, and gave Albert a kiss on the forehead.

"Dinner smells wonderful; what are you making?" Albert spun around like a tornado, almost knocking her down had she not been leaning against the counter. Victoria looked startled and paled.

"What the hell is going on?" Albert told the kids to fix a plate and watch TV. They both looked at him to see if this was a test. They were scared to move. It was the first time he gave them consent to do that.

"If you want dinner, I suggest you get it in two minutes and get out." They did what he told them to. The surprise on Victoria's face looked like he had just smashed an egg on her head. Her face was half shattered and half shocked. She took his hands.

"Sit and tell me what is going on?" He took a seat and a few long breaths. It felt like someone had put a pillow over his face, and he couldn't breathe. He looked up at her. "Your ex-husband, George called. He wants you to call him about Stacy. That is all he said before abruptly hanging up the phone." Feeling surreal and looking like she had seen a ghost, Victoria paled, and he took a seat beside her.

"That is all he said? It has been almost two years since I have heard from him."

"Yes, that is all he had to say." Victoria regained her composure and rushed to the phone. She then asked the operator to dial the international number. After what felt like a lifetime, he picked the phone up on the other end.

"Hello, this is George. Who is calling, please?" Victoria cleared her throat. Anger took over at the sound of his voice. The pure hate she felt for him when he took their kids was enough to send a rational person over the edge. Through her clenched teeth, she replied.

"This is Victoria. What did you call for, George?" In rapid fire, George spat out,

"Stacy is on his way to the states and needs to be picked up at the airport tomorrow around noon time at South West Florida International." then he told her about his nightmares and seeing ghosts. He continued with the flight numbers, layover schedule, and hung up. Victoria never said a word after his initial hello to George. Albert listened and wondered *what was being said on the other end of the line*. Victoria had appeared angry, then sad, and then shocked. It was a whirlwind of emotions that shared little to no answers. Hanging up the phone, Victoria took a seat. Albert had made her a scotch on the rocks. She took a long draw of the drink and felt it burn like fire all the way to her core. Then she took a breath.

"Stacy is on a plane on his way home, alone. I guess he struggled with nightmares and had been seeing ghosts. I don't know, he made little sense. So, he put him on a plane home." Albert plopped down onto the seat next to her. He felt like he weighed as much as an elephant. It was too much for him to handle. After all, he was already taking care of two of her kids. Victoria took another drink and filled him in on the details of the flight.

Stacy peered up at the lady stewardess with wide blue eyes and a look of fear on his face. She wore the standard uniform given to all the staff. When they approached where Stacy would sit, he looked around with caution. The plane was two stories, plenty of room for him to stretch if needed. The stale air smelled of musk and whisky. The lady buckled him in and busied herself helping other guests settle in. Coming back to him after the flight reached a specific altitude that allowed him to roam the plane. She offered him apple juice and wafers. He took them reluctantly and ate all but a few. For dinner, he was served sliced beef, mashed potatoes and mixed vegetables with milk. Stacy was scared; he hadn't spoken since he'd been dropped off to this lady. She unbuckled him and took his hand. She led the way to the facilities and showed Stacy. He understood and used the room to do his business. Returning to his seat, he fell fast asleep.

After dinner, they reached out to Uncle Brad and told him what had happened. He offered to keep the kids tomorrow to give Victoria time to get prepared for Stacy's arrival. Victoria, along with her friend Lindsey, would meet Stacy at the airport. After speaking with her brother, she called Lindsey to let her know they were all set for tomorrow. Lindsey would pick her up around ten in order to get to the airport in time to check through security and get to the gate. After they landed, a flight attendant escorted Stacy off the plane. Victoria recognized him immediately. She showed the lady her ID and looked at Stacy, who held a little suitcase and wore knickers. They terrified him; he did not know what was going on or who these people were. He wanted his daddy. Little tears ran down his face. Victoria and Lindsey tried to soothe him.

"Son, it'll be ok," Victoria said. Stacy shook his head no. He coiled into himself and was silent. He wanted to disappear. He was still crying when his mother bent down and looked him in the eyes.

"Come on, son, let's go home." No matter how Victoria or Lindsey tried to entice Stacy to talk, he wouldn't. Stacy felt lost and terrified. He shook and cried harder when they spoke to him. He sat as physically close to the car door as possible and buried his head in his hands as the tears continued to fall. It had been a scary four days of travel to his destiny, feeling terribly alone. Stacy occasionally looked out the window as the houses and cars whizzed by in super speed, like a wind whipping the sand in swirls during a windstorm. His heart felt deflated, and he ached for his dad to clear this up. Scared and lonely, like a lost kid. Tears rolled down his cheeks. He didn't say an entire word all the way to the Haas residence.

When they arrived, Stacy did not want to get out of the car. The house looked massive to him. Different from his home back in New Zealand. He looked around and quietly observed the kids and a man that was there. Victoria showed him what would be his room. He jumped on the bed and buried his face with his hands and cried. He did not like it here and was terrified of these people. He didn't understand why his life had so abruptly changed. Stacy had one toy from New Zealand, a stack and sort tower. Over the next few days, they would find him in his room. Sometimes he played with his little trinkets, and other times he cried. No one could break through to him.

He still did not talk for almost a week until one morning at breakfast. "Where's my daddy?" You could have heard a pin drop; it was so quiet. Robby laughed, and Donald followed suit. They both got smacked on the back of the head by Albert, which brought tears to their eyes. They quieted down quickly.

"Stacy, what did you say?" Victoria said. He repeated himself. They learned that although Stacy knew English, he spoke so quietly it was hard to hear and understand. He had chosen not to speak so far. When he refused to talk, he would resort to using hand signals. Using a grabbing motion along with balling a fist and hitting the top of the fist, they figured out meant he wanted the ketchup. They all knew that it was going to be a transition. That evening, with a fire burning, Albert and Victoria talked quietly. The older boys played. Stacy stayed in his room alone. There was a chill in the air despite the fire, like a gray night when a storm was approaching. Nothing Victoria could do made her feel warm. She worried about how things would work out. With eyes that usually shone, now dark, she turned to Albert.

"How are we going to do this?" He looked up from reading the paper to give her his full attention. "We will be alright; give him time.

He will adjust. Look at him. He seems to have an ok time with Robby." Victoria looked at the boys with an uncertain smile and shook her head. Stacy had come out of his room with his toy. Robby went over to play with him. She tried to convince herself that Albert was right. They would be ok. Still, she wondered what was about to come. As she looked off into the distance, she rose from her rocking chair that was her gramme's, the type that has the old wood that squeaked when you rock in it and retrieved another drink for the two of them. She handed him his drink.

"Should we postpone the wedding?" she asked.

"No, we shouldn't, everything will be fine."

Victoria went over and checked on the boys. She told them it was time for lights out. The boys went to put on their pajamas and brush their teeth. Once they were in bed, Stacy heard Albert approaching his room. He buried his face under the covers as he glanced in. Albert knew it was time to get him enrolled in kindergarten. The next morning, Victoria got him ready and headed over to the school. The elementary school was down across the street from their house. Stacy still felt alone and did not know if this new life was going to last or not. It relieved Stacy that he would be somewhere besides that house. The school placed him in preschool to see what he knew. They tested his knowledge on his A, B, C's and his numbers. Upon the testing, the school determined after two weeks that he was ready for kindergarten. Stacy gradually came out of his shell at school. It was not home; he enjoyed it and preferred it. He made friends quickly, and the teachers loved him. When school was out for a hurricane or a holiday, he stayed to himself.

A friend taught him how to tie his shoes and say his first curse word, "Shit," that year in kindergarten. He got in trouble when he said the word at home. He had not realized it was a dirty word. Home life was still scary, and he tried to stay out of trouble. The rules were so strict, it was hard for his little mind to take it all in and remember all of them. One day, he got into trouble for running down the street to school alone. He was so proud of himself; he was a big boy now. Albert knocked the pride right out of him when he got to him.

"I cannot believe you crossed the street alone." Stacy stood there, chest out, arms crossed; he was proudly showing the start of his independence. Getting scolded, he looked at his stepdad.

"I did it alone; I'm sorry."

"We'll deal with this after school." he marched back across the busy street in front of their home. He could hear him slam the door. Head down, shoulders hanging low; four-year-old Stacy, hating him, continued his walk to class.

"Good Morning, Stacy." His kindergarten teacher said. He looked up with little tears, waiting to escape with a warm smile.

"Good Morning." He replied while he took his seat. All he could think about that day was what he was in trouble for and the consequences that afternoon. When school ended, he saw his stepdad waiting for him out front. He grabbed his arm and almost drug him home. His little arm was red. It hurt from his grip on the way home. Quietly, he walked along beside him.

"You will go without a snack. Go to your room; no playing today either."

Then he smacked him across his face. Crying now, Stacy went to his room and played alone with his trinket from New Zealand. For such a young child, he spent too much time isolated. Stacy feared for his life, confused at the turn of events. He found solace nowhere.

Most times, he could be found, if they wanted to find him, alone somewhere within the walls of what felt like a prison. His small face and tiny body were easily overlooked for the most part. If he was quiet and did not move around much, he wasn't missed. He could go hours without any adult supervision or contact. Some days, in the beginning, he would show up in the kitchen hours after a meal, hungry. They had forgotten he was even there and neglected to call him to the table to eat. He lost weight and looked unhealthy, ghostly white, his skin matching his light blonde hair. One day he went all day without eating during the winter break. He played alone in his room and was entirely forgotten about.

No one ever apologized for this oversight; it was as if it was on him to speak up and be heard. On the occasion he did speak up it was always the wrong time, and he would get punished with a piece of wood from the beach a whack to the side of the head, making his ears ring.

"Stacy, what the hell are you doing?" Albert said. Stacy was standing in the kitchen shoveling some crackers in his mouth. His mouth, full and dry from the crackers, caused him to choke as he tried to answer him. As he gagged and spit up crackers all over the floor, Albert grew furious.

"I am hungry," Stacy spat out. Albert grabbed him by the shirt, and with a tongue lashing like he'd never heard, he marched him up to the bathroom. He washed him up, then made him stand there while he continued to lash out. When he was spent, he reached over and spanked him so hard on his legs it left welts. Stacy never ate without asking again after that day. On other occasions, Stacy would go missing for hours in his own home. He was so small it was easy for him to disappear in plain sight. He hid in the far corner of his room behind the dresser for hours it seemed. He grew tired of hiding, so he emerged; he had not known they were looking for him. He had become engrossed in playing with his trinket. "Where have you been! I've searched this place high and low. You missed lunch again. What is wrong with you?" Albert fired at him like bullets. Stacy stood still as he wished he could become invisible again. He found himself being pushed into a chair facing the wall, being held there as Albert crushed him into the wall. He did not squirm, knowing this would make things worse. After he was released, he was excused only to go to his room, with a warning he better see him if he came looking.

There were other adults that observed this behavior from Alberts, so Stacy began to think this was the way it was supposed to be. He did not go many places outside of school and his home; there were no role models for what life in America was about. He knew he wasn't abused in New Zealand, but he thought his dad had disappeared one day. He vaguely remembers being on an airplane. When Lindsey visited them, he would tell Stacy about the day her and his mom had picked Stacy up from the airport. Stacy liked to hear her stories, but he could not connect the dots on how he ended up with this family, with the horrible man that ruled the house. Stacy never talked about how he was treated. He thought he had been the one who did something wrong. None of the adults that witnessed this abuse stood up and objected. Stacy eventually started calling Albert dad since all the others did, and he was the only dad he could remember.

THREE

STACY WAS NOW FIVE YEARS OLD AND IN THE FIRST GRADE.

Throughout the last year, his anger grew as he became more alienated by these people. Anger boiled deep in his soul like water ready to boil over in a pot. He lived day to day in fear and anger. Even though Stacy participated in school, the teaching staff knew he was building walls. He never participated unless called upon. He did not join others on the playground during morning recess. Alone, by the fence, playing with the rocks is where you could find Stacy most days during this time. He was never rude to the kids or staff; he simply didn't speak unless someone spoke to him first. There was a quiet demeanor to him that could not be penetrated yet. When asked a question on a topic of study, Stacy answered the question correctly every time. He was a smart, serious young man. No one could quite put their finger on what was going on with him. He was more private and to himself than a hermit would be.

He kicked rocks around after school simply because he didn't want to go home. As he waited for his stepdad to escort him across the street, another rock hit the side of the road. His hands were buried deep in his pockets as a rock skipped across the pavement. He hung his head low as he saw him standing there waiting on him irritably. The street was busy as they raced across it. He reached for the gate rushing inside. Stacy went to his room until he was told it was dinner time. Everyone except Albert had already sat down at the table. Stacy looked around and noticed the only seat left was a seat beside him. Panic stricken, he started to fidget.

"Mom, I don't want to sit next to him. I'm afraid of him." He whispered.

"You don't want to sit next to me? Fine. Eat outside in the heat out of this dog bowl," he replied as he returned from the kitchen. He had obviously heard the conversation. Turning red from being caught and embarrassed. Stacy sat on the deck floor eating out of a dog bowl. It humiliated him beyond words. While the rest of them ate at the table and talked, he sat out there, lost. His food went untouched as he stared at the ocean. He sat silently listening to Albert and his mom have a conversation about their day. Albert complained about the kids he always did.

"They don't listen, none of them," he said.

"They are in school all day; you don't have them that long, Albert," Victoria replied.

Albert slammed his fork down on the table and glared at her.

"Go to hell!" he said. Victoria shook her head and returned her focus to eating. He picked up his fork and slowly started to eat again.

"You should be with them." he made the simple statement. However, Victoria didn't take the bait. They had plenty of money and no need for either to work. He was here most days when school ended. She had a social life to attend to. Stacy wondered *why his mom hadn't stuck up for him. She always let him get away with hurting him.* A knock at their door interrupted them. Victoria went to answer it.

"Hi, Carol, Jack, come on in. We're just finishing dinner." They were friends of theirs and often came over to play cards. When they entered the dining room, they saw Stacy instantly on the deck with a dog bowl. He was eating on the floor. His body went limp, and he wished he could melt into the planks, like a candle that was lit, melting under the heat. In pure disbelief, with a look of bewilderment, Carol said quickly,

"We'll wait in the living room." They retraced their steps and sat open mouthed. Moments that felt like hours passed when Stacy came in and asked, "May I be excused?" Victoria lifted her head and looked down at him.

"Yes, you can." He put his dog bowl in the sink as tears streamed down his face. He ran to his room, slamming the door, and buried his head. Never in his life could he remember a time that embarrassed him as much. He wondered if he'd have stayed in New Zealand if it would have been the same. He wondered what he had done to be shipped here to these people. He always tried figuring out what was wrong with him. He covered up his head and slowly drifted off to sleep.

The next morning, he woke abruptly; he found himself wet. Embarrassed that he had wet the bed at five years old, he rushed to the bathroom and changed clothes. "Why is the bed wet?" Albert asked as he gave him a laundry basket of clothes. Feeling the warmth sweep over him, he turned red. He looked up at Albert, who towered over him.

"I guess I must have wet the bed." He knocked the basket out of Stacy's hands, then took his jaw in his hand and squeezed it.

"I guess you'll be wearing a pull up tonight."

"No, dad, please. It was an accident." His tears threatened to spill over. He knew if he allowed them to escape, he would be in more trouble. He quickly gathered his things and headed to school. He ran as fast as his little legs would allow, across the street to safety. School was a blur that day. He kept remembering the night before and eating off the floor. He also worried about what this evening would bring. He was terrified he would have to wear a diaper to bed like a baby. Sure enough, that evening, in front of his brother's, Albert put a pull up on him. His face blowing up and turning red with anger, he said to Albert in a deep, dark voice that sounded foreign to his own ears,

"I hate you." As he ran off, he could hear the other boys, supposedly his brothers, laughing at him. He felt like he would explode with hatred for him and this family. This would be one of many moments that would scar him forever. He would not easily forget all the shaming he received or the punishments. Which no one deserves. He only hoped, even at this young age, that one day he would be free and left alone. He tired quickly from pure self-hate and fell asleep.

That year was one of learning, patience and adjustments. Stacy had joined them over a year ago. He had come a long way, but Albert thought *he had a long way to go*. His mission with the boys was that they knew he had total control. He demanded it, even from Victoria. There were days at the dinner table, if Stacy didn't hold his fork properly, he'd grab his neck and squeeze it, leaving it red. The only things he enjoyed were school and spending time at Gramme's house. It was a hot day for Florida, with temperatures in the upper 90's. The kids were restless, hot, and complained a lot. The beaches were crowded, and Albert was trying to pack for their month-long family vacation at Marco Island.

He dropped the laundry basket in frustration, which made all the boys jump at the loud noise. "You damn kids are driving me crazy. Get out of the house and go play! Do not get into any trouble or else." Stacy tripped over the clothes basket on his way to the door. He reached out and smacked him. His face instantly sported a red hand-print; the smack was so sudden and hard that he had jarred his teeth, he cried.

"Boys don't cry. Dry it up right now, or you'll be in real trouble." He thought *he looked like the ugliest monster he could imagine*. His hair was a mess from packing and cleaning, and his shirt stained from where he'd cooked lunch. Stacy's shoulders sank, and he bowed his head. He was afraid to move, so he stood and held his breath while he waited for more.

"Go, get out. Go to your room." Afraid to do anything but what he was told. He hurried to his room. His face burned with the slap as he rubbed it. Albert expected Victoria to be home at any moment. He rushed around to complete his task of packing. So, he could have his drink ready. The thing about Albert and that there was no need to work, was because Victoria had family money. She was filthy rich, which in turn made Albert her little bitch. The front door flew open and hit the wall behind it. Startled, he jumped and turned around in a fury.

"What the hell." he yelled. Immediately, he felt embarrassed and apologized to Lindsey.

"I am sorry. I went to knock, and the door opened. The wind whipped it out of my hand. I didn't mean to startle you."

"No, I'm sorry. I overreacted; the kids were getting under my skin today and I am trying to get packed for vacation before Victoria gets home. Please come in. Can I get you a drink?"

Lindsey shook her head as she closed the door. "Sure. How about a bourbon? Neat, please." Albert smiled as he gave her a hug and ran along to get her a drink. She took a seat.

She then spied Stacy, who sat on the bottom step, as close to the wall as he could. He could have been a picture hanging there. He looked so small and fragile. Lindsey grinned. "Stacy, come sit with me." Slowly, like a scared little kitten, not sure if it was safe, Stacy went over to her. Lindsey lifted him up to sit on her lap, Stacy relaxed. She thought she felt like Stacy could finally breathe as she felt him relax on her lap. Stacy loved when Lindsey came to visit. He remembered when he first met her not so long ago at the airport.

"Are you going on vacation with us?" Stacy whispered. She smiled.

"No, but I am coming down for Labor Day. I would not miss the clambake." Stacy nodded. He could not wait until the clambake now. He feared the adults he ended up living with. Moments later, Albert reentered the room with a drink in his hand. He took it over to Lindsey.

"Stacy, get down. Run along and play. Leave our guest alone." He had such an intimidating, hateful voice. Like he spit out the words. Stacy stiffened up again.

"He is fine. I told him to come sit with me." She then tickled him.

Stacy laughed until tears roll down his cheeks and he could not catch his breath. He rarely laughed.

One reason he liked when Lindsey was around. She took a sip of her drink, then looked at Stacy.

"Thanks for keeping me company buddy now go play." Stacy did as he was told. He went to his room and got out his trinkets from New Zealand and his dad. He sadly wondered *how he had died. He had asked where his dad was often. Until, one day, they had told him he was gone. From that moment on, he thought, gone meant dead.* George was still alive and well in New Zealand. Like a boy that lost his puppy, he sat there and looked at the trinkets. He remembered *when his dad and Donald would take him to the park or to a castle.* He loved his grandmother, too. After a while, he grew sleepy and jumped about five feet to get to his bed. Stacy thought there were boogeymen under his bed. That is why he always jumped from so far away.

Stacy dreamed of his grandma that night. He woke abruptly to the sound of laughter. He ground his little fists on his eyes to remove the sleep out of them. Then crawled out from under his blanket. With a look of curiosity on his face, he listened at the top of the stairs to see who was there. He heard his stepdad, mom, and Uncle Brad. Carefully, he walked down the steps.

He had a flashback of when he fell while running down the stairs; he was more cautious now. He had set his stepdad off when he fell and learned to be careful. As he entered the living room, he did not see anyone. He went to the kitchen. Finding all of them around the table. His stepdad looked up. "Well, I am sure glad you could make it to dinner on time." He hissed like a snake ready to bite.

Embarrassed again, Stacy dropped his head. "Sorry, dad." Albert directed him to the kitchen to make a peanut butter sandwich. His punishment for being late to dinner. While he ate his sandwich alone in the kitchen, he felt invisible. He still could not understand why he had to be with these people. He grew lonelier by the day. Even though he was too young to know what loneliness truly was. The yearning he felt in the pit of his stomach told him something was off.

He didn't know what it meant exactly. He finished his sandwich and walked around the dining room to avoid the stares and went to bed. He was crushed as if the walls had swallow him up like the gigantic wave that once knocked him down and his dad had to reach in to save him. He was still terrified of these people. It was this year Stacy found out his actual dad was not dead. George had sent his brother to live with them until his return. Donald, almost eight now; had a returned to his home to the states. He realized the major differences and learned to comply quickly. Elsie had hit the teen years and her defiance, caused havoc for everyone in the house.

"Elsie, stop it right now," Albert said. Elsie was making something to eat.

"Why can't I have something to eat?"

"Because, dinner is in a few hours, and lunch is over. Because I said so."

Elsie made a wrinkled face with an eye roll, "Well, that's ridiculous; I'm hungry." Elsie said, as she continued to make her sandwich.

"I said stop it right now." Albert's voice was sharp. He grabbed Elsie by the hair and drug her out of the kitchen. Elsie sent shrewd remarks back at him along the way.

"You are evil; why are you doing this? I should take my siblings and leave," she whined.

Albert grew more frustrated by the minute, slamming the door behind Elsie as he went outside. Under his breath, Albert swore and *thought that girl needs a good ass beating and mouth full of soap.* After that, Elsie went outside to mother Stacy. She followed him around everywhere. She tried to take care of him. He was not used to this kind of attention, and he didn't like it. He wanted nothing to do with her and wanted to be left alone.

"Stacy, I wish I could take you and raise you. I would treat you like a baby. You don't deserve to be treated like this. That man is wretched," she continued. Stacy looked like a lost boy as he looked around to see where he could escape to. He did not need her complicating things. Her mothering him was as bad as the abuse he received from Albert. Desperate to escape them, Stacy started hiding in the far corner of his bed. He found solace there or in the corner of their yard, behind a stone wall. He played for hours, but with diligence, Elsie always found him. She was the one that took him to the table to eat. She insisted on bathing him, tucking him in. It was all too much for Stacy. He started lashing out more often.

"Leave me alone!" he yelled at Elsie one afternoon. Albert came into the living room where the commotion came from.

"What's going on, Stacy?" He looked between Albert and Elsie and wondered why he was being targeted.

"I want her to leave me alone." He said, emphasizing each word through gritted teeth. His small hands in fists and his face turning bright red. Albert turned to Elsie,

"You heard him. Leave him alone or else." Elsie stood there with her mouth dropped open.

"Or else what?" she finally blurted out. Albert took her by the head and marched her to the corner.

"Or else you will stand here for thirty minutes with me pushing your nose to the wall, instead of twenty minutes on your own." Albert had won that battle, he thought as he walked away from a crying Elsie. Soon enough, over the weeks, once Elsie figured out she could undermine Albert, the war began. It was a battle of will, which Albert grew tired of fast. His tolerance for Elsie was zero; he could not stand that child. He often complained to Victoria. She took the high road for a while and grew tired of him always complaining the minute she walked in the door.

Over the next few months between Robby and Elsie. Both older than the other boys did not comply with the rules and became defiant. Albert threw his hands up in the air in frustration.

"Victoria, it's Elsie or me. I can't take anymore. She goes, or I go, you decide." He said, one afternoon.

"Ok, I'll send her back to live with her dad. I cannot take anymore either." It was only a few days later that Elsie left with all her belongings. She cried at the door, saying bye to her siblings.

None of the boys particularly felt sad; they barely knew her. What they did know is the hell they lived in daily got a lot hotter when she arrived. Unfortunately, no one was sad to see her go. Each of them had their own battles to overcome and did not need the added distractions. As odd as it might appear, the house that was anything but normal went back to the normal Albert demanded. Victoria had told George she was dropping Elsie off; he had moved back to the states a month after he sent Elsie back. Although he had visitation with all of them, he never attempted to gain custody of any of them. It confused Stacy; it took him a while to understand this stranger was his dad. He didn't enjoy going there, and often as he got older, he would make plans with his friend. This kept him from having to go.

Albert was so relieved that Elsie would not be joining them on Marco Island; he was in a good mood for an entire afternoon. Stacy almost laughed at him singing as he covered his mouth, so he would not think he was laughing at him. He saw him standing in the doorway and handed him a warm cookie.

"Here, enjoy. I'm in a good mood and making these for the beach. Now run along before my mood changes." Albert warned, and Stacy took the cookie like a bird, so gentle and left the room. Stacy didn't get to go far this year at the beach; he was too young. This made him the root of Albert's frustration, and he spared nothing, taking it out on him. Every weekend his parents showed up and Victoria would remind the boys to be scarce. In other words, stay out of the way as he intended to do.

While at the beach, Stacy remembered very little. He was so young, he spent most of his time either under the umbrella, being made to stay, like a puppy being trained not to move. He remembers all the times he was smacked or made to stand in the corner. He also remembers Albert laid out in the sun like a sun worshiper from 10 o'clock in the morning until 3 o'clock in the afternoon. Robby thought *Alberts long bleached hair, and tanning was as odd as it got.*

"Stacy don't sling the sand everywhere," Albert complained one afternoon. Stacy looked over to him, his face blushing. He was hot and wanted to go in the water.

"I'm hot." He glared at him.

"Are you complaining or whining?" He shook his head back and forth

"No," he laid back down on his blanket beside Victoria, while she read a book. He tanned. A few more moments passed when Robby appeared.

"Can I take Stacy down to the water's edge to cool off?" With a huff once again, Albert sat up.

"Yes, he drowns it's on you," was all he said as he laid back down. Stacy hopped up, happy to be able to get wet; his face was flushed from being overheated. Robby took his hand and said,

"Grab that ring." Stacy did, and they were off. He sat halfway in the water and the sand. He laughed as the bubbling water would splash on him. The ring securely around his waist. Each wave knocked him over and he squealed in delight. Robby played nearby; he was riding the waves and crashing on the shore. Stacy could not remember having a better time. The water rushing over his hot body felt so refreshing. Once or twice, he coughed as a wave hit him square in the mouth; he had swallowed a lot of sea water that day. By dinner time, Stacy was out like a light. His day had been full of sun and water, which tired him quickly. He slept through to the next morning. Stacy also remembers the fires and the fireworks on Labor Day. One of the most extraordinary things he had seen so far in his young years. He danced and pointed, tugged at Robby's hand in excitement. Robby was glad he offered to take him to the water's edge. This behavior was sure to put Albert over the edge. Robby had saved Stacy from a vast amount of abuse that summer by suggesting he take Stacy to tag along.

FOUR

STACY WAS NOW SIX YEARS OLD AND IN THE SECOND GRADE.

The school year was ending; it had flown by as Stacy became more engaged this year. Not that he made many friends, but he poured himself into learning. He was a smart kid. His favorite subject was history. He wasn't sure why; he just liked to pretend he lived in a different time or place. Of course, that became a common theme for him during his second year of living in the states with this family. There was more of the same with Albert, the drill Sargent, that also delivered corporal punishment. Not a day passed that Stacy's anxiety level was normal or stable. His anxiety was crippling some days. The thought of going home or being with Albert was suffocating. He would pull at his hair and violently twist his fingers together to feel alive. He was unnoticed so often unless he wasn't, and that was a torture chamber.

Stacy had made a friend; his name was Shaun. They played base-ball together that year. They became inseparable.

"Stacy, want to come and spend the weekend?" Shaun asked. Stacy grinned from ear to ear with excitement.

"Yes, I will ask my dad tonight." The two of them often spent most of their time playing at the park or at Shaun's house. His parents were nice, and Stacy felt safe there. After school, he ran home to catch his dad. He preferred to deal with his mom, but she insisted he deal with his dad. He ran into the house like a rush of wind. The house smelled of fresh clam chowder soup, which made his mouth water with the scent of creamy sauce in the air. As he entered the kitchen, he saw his mom at the sink. "Is dad home yet?" Not looking up from doing the dishes, Victoria shook her head no. A few minutes went by. Stacy went outside to wait for his dad. After what felt like an eternity to him, he saw his dad drive up. He did not wait for him to get out of the car before he ran over to where he parked.

"Dad, Shaun wants to know if I can spend the weekend at his house. Can I?" His dad got out of the car and, with a shrug,

"Why the hell do I care?"

"Does that mean yes?"

"YES!" Albert barked. Stacy skipped back to the house. He went up to his room and packed his bag. It was hard for him to fall asleep that night. Finally, he gave in and fell asleep. The next morning, Stacy got up and dressed. He preferred to get out of the house before his stepdad got up. As he tiptoed to the kitchen, he realized he was not up yet. Quiet as a mouse, he made himself some cereal. He ate it like a hungry dog. He washed the bowl like he had taught him. He rushed out the door with his bag.

"Hey, wait up Shaun," Stacy yelled. Shaun turned to look at him and stopped walking as Stacy jogged over to him.

"Did they say you could stay over this weekend?"

"Yes, they did." Both wore big smiles as they walked to their classroom.

After school, the boys rushed over to Shaun's, running through the door like a storm. Shaun's house sat right beside Stacy's. He could cut through their backyard to hang out with him.

"Hi guys, how was school?" Mrs. Anders said. Shaun's mom stood there with her hands on her hips, beaming.

"It was great, mom. Can we get in the pool?"

"Sure, but I have fresh chocolate chip cookies if you want a snack first." Both boys foamed at the mouth. They agreed on a snack first. Stacy had the best time. There were no insults, no smacks, or objects being thrown at him. They ate together and laughed and joked through dinner. It was his safe place.

Stacy had completed the second grade. He was not happy that he had to go to the beach; he wanted to stay home and play baseball. He asked his parents several times to come watch a practice or a game. They had never shown up. The next morning everyone rose early, there was excitement in the air, and it was the day they left for vacation. Stacy got up when he heard Donald. Otherwise, he might miss breakfast with the family. The older he got, the more intuitive, resourceful and smart he became. Only through punishment had he wised up a little. Victoria hummed in the kitchen while making breakfast when he walked in. "Good Morning," she said. Stacy nodded without a word. He ran out to help set the table and escape. It took him longer to realize there was no escaping his dad. He entered the dining room and hit him with a wooden clothes hanger.

"When your mother says Good Morning, I expect a response. Not a nod, and you runoff. Understand me?" Albert said.

"Yes, sir." Today for breakfast, they had ham and eggs with toast, butter, and jelly. Stacy's favorite was strawberry. They ate and cleared the table while Victoria washed the dishes and Albert loaded the car. The boys chased each other around outside. All loaded, Victoria yelled for the boys,

"let's go," as they came running and jumped in the car. Donald helped Stacy in and shut the door. They stopped to fill up with gas. Victoria gave them 25 cents to go get a gumball, another rarity. Stacy doesn't like gumballs ever since he swallowed one, and Albert caught him. After that, every time he had gum, he made him spit it out in his hand. Gross. Now he always got some hard candy.

Once at Marco Island, they looked for a house called "By the sea." Stacy didn't understand why a house had a name. They found the house, and it was "By the sea," the sand is right at the house's back door. It was an enormous house. *Like three times the size of their house,* Stacy thought. This was only Stacy's second visit to the Island. His siblings have been for several years while he was in New Zealand. He bubbled over with excitement, finding it hard to contain himself. All three boys jumped out of the car and started running for the sand.

"Stop right this minute," Albert yelled. The three of them stopped like they had run into a brick wall. They stood frozen in place.

"First things first, let's unload the car. We still need to get our rooms set up. Put swimsuits on, and then we will head to the beach." They ran back to the car to help unload. Heads hung low, with frowning faces.

The older brothers knew when they finished, the rule was, play where I can see but not hear you. It was one of the freest times they got while living with Albert. They cherished it. They got dirty, played in the sand, buried each other. They jumped the waves as they crashed onto the beach. It was a good time for them. Stacy learned early on that this vacation time was for Victoria and Albert, not the family. They were just there, by no choice of Albert's. While Albert carried the cooler, Robby carried the chairs down to the beach. Victoria followed behind them with the towels.

"Run along now and play. Tell your brother the rules too." Victoria said. They ran and threw a ball to each other. Stacy played in the sand, but the boys neglected to tell him what the rules were. He dug deep holes in the sand, built sandcastles that looked more like mounds of sand. But he smiled. He dipped his feet in the water as it rushed up to his knees. He squealed with delight, running away from the waves. He collected shells and took them to put on his towel to take home with him.

"Hey! What do you think you are doing? Did you not listen to the rules?" Albert said.

Stacy tensed up and wondered what he had done.

"Nobody told me the rules."

"No one told you the rules," Albert corrected his grammar. He shook his head.

"Well, ask then," he said. Stacy turned to walk away, frustrated.

"Did I dismiss you? Take those shells back and throw them in the water. We do not take the shells from nature." Albert raised his voice.

"Okay." Stacy retrieved the shells and wandered back to the water. He threw each one as a tear rolled down his face. His last one was his favorite. He snuck and put it in his shorts pocket. Feeling it there, he smiled. He found the rules to be confusing. He figured he should probably stay close to Donald, so he wouldn't get in trouble. While Victoria laid in the sun, she read the latest beach read book she had brought. She thought, *this is heaven.* She loved to sunbathe. They had been going there for three years now. They had to change houses since the other rental was sold and taken off the vacation rental pool. She had to admit the place was gorgeous. With its three stories, a hot tub, outdoor shower, shaker siding, a kitchen to die for and two living rooms, one with games downstairs, the other next to the kitchen.

The boys could have the downstairs game room. She can monitor them while having a bonfire if they did not want to join, she thought to herself. Victoria looked down at her watch and figured she needed to give the kids lunch. She called out to them to come have lunch. As they came running, Albert got the sandwiches out of the ice chest and laid them on a napkin. He placed them on their towels. The boys made short time eating. Anyone who watched would think they had not eaten in a week. Albert scolded them and told them to slow down. They had to wait 30 minutes before going into the water. An old wives tale he believed in, regarding swimming right after you ate. They slowed down. They all said sorry. After they finished, the three of them made a sandcastle with their mom to let their food settle and let Albert enjoy sunbathing.

He laid down with his headset on and rolled over and fell asleep soaking up the sun. Stacy yawned. Because he still got cranky without a quick nap, his mom laid him under the umbrella on his towel with his blanket. He fell asleep almost instantly. Victoria knew this would be a great opportunity to take the older boys fishing. They loved to fish off the pier. She grabbed the tackle box, bait and fishing poles. They headed towards the pier. As they walked near the water, the waves rolled across their feet. Victoria smelled the salty air, and the warm sun brought peace. She carefully taught Donald how to bait his hook without getting the hook stuck in his hand. Then showed him how to cast the pole. Robby was an expert at fishing and already had his line in the water. It was still early in the season, so there were very few people around.

It was nice to have an almost empty beach and pier. Victoria knew that come July 4th; people would flood in like sardines. The firework displays and festivities would bring the people. Each year there were huge bonfires, clambakes and beer. They took part in the festivities as well. The way the beach curved you could see huge bonfires for miles. It was beautiful to see.

"Mom, I'm bored. I don't like to fish; can I go back to the beach?" Donald said. Victoria shook her head and wondered what boy did not like to fish. She told him to go near where his dad was and not in the water until he was awake, or they got back.

About that time,

"I got one!" Robby said. Donald turned and ran away as he rolled his eyes. Robby worked hard to reel in the fish. It was a big one. He got it off the hook.

"Congratulations! You just caught dinner," Victoria said. The wind picked up as the sun set. Victoria and Robby packed up and headed back to the others. "Thanks, mom," Robby said.

"Anytime."

Stacy ran to meet up with her and Robby halfway back to where they were.

"Hi, did you catch anything? Donald told me you went fishing. Mom, I want to go one day." Shaking her head ok, Victoria handed the tackle box to Stacy to carry. He felt like such a big boy carrying the tackle box. Stacy respected his mom, though she shared little emotion, rules, or anything. He knew his mom tried where his stepdad did not.

"I'm going to take a quick shower and start prepping for dinner. Want me to bring you a cocktail?" Victoria said as they reached where Albert sat.

"Yes," he said. She made a drink for him and one for herself. Smiling, she handed him the drink.

"I'm thinking we'll go light tonight with some burgers and dogs along with chips."

"I'll grill the meat. I have pasta salad we can have with it as well. We can save the chips for lunch," she said. Stacy grew tired and returned to the house. He knew he couldn't hang out with his mom. He went to his room and played after he let his mom know where he would be. Victoria prepared dinner. When the burgers were almost ready to come off the grill, she went over to Stacy's door.

"Go tell your dad dinner is ready." Stacy ran down the little trail to the beach.

"Dinner is ready." His dad and brothers showed up in no time, and they all walked back to the house. Victoria told the older boys to shower,

"one of you outside, the other on the inside. You can switch tomorrow." They decided between the two of them who was first to use the outside shower. In the meantime, she ran bath water for Stacy and submerged him in nice, warm water. It was still a little chilly on his skin, which had turned pink from the sun. He splashed around a bit, got out, dried off and put his pajamas on, and joined everyone on the deck.

After they ate, it was time to watch the sunset, and if they were lucky, some lightning bugs would be out for them to catch. The boys made friends with both neighbor's kids and started a game of kickball in the side yard. Although Stacy was the youngest and could not quite kick the ball, they let him go to first base. Stacy whined as he grew tired. Robby bent down.

"Don't whine, buddy. If you are tired and don't want to play, that's fine. Go sit with mom and dad or go to bed, okay?" Stacy agreed and ran up to his mom.

"Mom, I'm tired. I'm going to bed." He laid his head on his pillow and fell fast asleep. Stacy dreamed of his days in New Zealand. He still didn't understand why he was being made to stay with this family. His heart ached; he felt so empty and alone; he wanted this dad, not the man everyone said was his dad. Finally, after several hours of playing, Victoria called the other boys in for the night. She told them not to wake Stacy. It didn't take long for any of them to fall asleep. It had been a long day. Victoria remembered seeing Stacy for the first time. Which reminded her to share the stuff he'd brought back with him from New Zealand. They stored away it in her hope chest back home. They spent lazy days at the beach in the water or playing in the sand. Most days were like their first day there, and it became routine.

They all looked forward to weekends when Lindsey came down and the 4th of July. This created a buffer for them since Albert would be in prep mode and better behavior. He would have less time to abuse or criticize them. Robby had already become rebellious. He would sneak out, smoke and drink if he could get his hands on them. Donald just complied with Albert. He did as he expected and did not make any waves. He'd learned early on to just suck up to him, and he'd be in good shape. As the summer progressed, there were no major issues or incidents which pleased Albert. What he hadn't realized was the boys had somewhat learned if they stayed away from him, they couldn't get in trouble. However, he set some rules. The one they hated the most was every day they had to look around and under rocks to find sharks teeth for their mother. This kept them busy. Weekends came and went. The 4th of July was this weekend, and Victoria planned for the festivities.

She quickly grabbed a pen and paper and started a to do list and a shopping list.

To do list

Grocery Shop

Have boys dig a deep hole in sand

Liquor Store

Party Store

Clean

Have boys clean deck area

Have boys bring up some rocks

Have boys get seaweed

Grocery list

Onions

Watermelon

Water

Italian bread

Butter

Napkins

Paper plates

Plastic ware

Tonic water

Fresh green leaf lettuce

Cucumbers

Tomatoes

Party Store

Streamers

Banner

Balloons

Flags

Sparklers

Feeling satisfied with her progress, Victoria made herself a gin and tonic. Then returned to the porch to relax in the afternoon breeze. Covered in muddy sand from head to toe, looking like one of the lost boys in a bad *Netflix* show, Stacy ran up to the deck. Albert, in frustration, glared at him and barked out orders to rinse off before he took another step. Robby took him over to the outside shower and turned the water on for him. Because everyone should know, especially his dad, that Stacy could not reach the nozzle. He rolled his eyes and made a snarly face towards Albert, aware that he could not see him behind the wall. That made Stacy laugh. And he did the same. Later that evening, after dinner, the boys played a board game while Stacy played with his Star Wars figures. It was a cool, rainy evening, so they played inside. Stacy turned to Albert with that same look Robby showed him by accident earlier. Albert looked at him, stunned.

"What do you think you're doing? Why would you dare make a face at me and roll your eyes?" Humiliated, hurt and confused because it was funny this afternoon, Stacy shook in fear of what would happen next. Albert got up and took his prized Star Wars figures. He grabbed him by the arm while his nails dug into his fragile skin and swatted him on the butt, demanding he go to bed for the night. In tears of anger, Stacy ran to his room, chanting under his breath, I hate you; I hate you; I hate you.

The next morning, while Victoria attended to the kids, Albert went to the store. Stacy's eyes were puffy and red from crying himself to sleep, and he was in a terrible mood. He wanted nothing to do with anyone. He wanted to be left alone. He realized for the first time, all he really wanted was to be alone. He didn't want to be hurt. He didn't want to be with him or any of them. While everyone played at the beach, he wandered off and enjoyed the loneliness that set in as he played on the rocks. It felt free, and slowly he embraced the loneliness. His mom looked around and spotted him playing on the rocks. she thought *at least he could preoccupy himself and he was in sight.* She passed a water to Robby, then settled back into working on the hole for the clambake.

"Go gather some rocks to go around the outside of the hole. Don't knock over that pile of sand; we'll need it tonight," she said to them. They both did as directed; Donald whined because he thought Stacy should help. For once, everyone let Stacy be because they all felt he got a raw deal most of the time and got in trouble for everything with Albert. Happy that he was out for most of the day, they accomplished all their tasks and now enjoyed the water and rode the waves. Stacy joined the other two in the water. They rode the waves to shore, which gave all of them scratched up bellies from the sandy shelly shore. Victoria hung the decorations Albert had bought. Then went to check on the potatoes. She was making potato salad and some clam chowder soup to go along with dinner. Preparation was everything to her. She lined the sandy walkway to the beach with little flags, hung the streamers and banner on the back deck that faced the ocean. The balloons would mark their clambake spot in the sand.

Satisfied with the way everything looked, she finished up the salad and soup. The clams were in the icebox, keeping chilled with seaweed over them for moisture. There was plenty of time to prep the bread and set tables. She decided on a cocktail of scotch neat, then headed out to see the boys. She noticed their war scratches from the waves and told them she didn't want to hear any complaining later when it stung during baths. They all nodded in unison and ran off to play some more, Robby and Donald in one direction and Stacy in another. He went back to the rocks, where he could once again be alone. He glanced back. He could see his parents alone; they were talking. He wondered, *what they were talking about.*

As they looked in his direction, he turned his back and bent down to play with the rocks. Stacy felt, if I can't see them, maybe I'll be invisible to them. He looked up at the house. He was excited about tonight's clam bake. He had never been to one. It looked festive and fun; he hoped he was right. The lights turned on at dusk to guide others to the beach. The Haas family grabbed the clams, an ice chest full of drinks along with appetizers, and headed to the beach.

They all helped lay out two large blankets. They set up five chairs. Victoria put out cheese and crackers, raw little necks with spicy sauce, fresh shrimp cocktail, along with a cheese fondue to dip bread in. Finally, Albert got the fire going in the hole they had dug earlier that day. They waited while the embers were getting ready to throw the clams on. Meanwhile, they sent the kids out to gather seaweed; it took them three trips to get enough. After the first trip and Albert yelled at them to bring more next time, they doubled up as much as they could. Little Stacy couldn't carry much, but he worked hard helping his brothers fill the buckets quickly. On their last trip getting seaweed, Stacy found a piece of a shark tooth, a rare one, it wasn't black like most of the ones they find, it was blue.

He put it in his pocket; he wanted to keep this too. He hoped he remembers to take it out before his dad washes the clothes and puts it with the seashell. Otherwise Albert will be mad and he won't get to keep it. He's a little bored, wondering when he will get his Star Wars figures back.

"Mom, can I go over there and play on the rocks?" Stacy said.

"Sure, but only for a few minutes, there's no light over there, and it'll be completely dark soon. Donald, why don't you go with him.". Donald nodded, and they headed over to the rocks to play. Even though Donald was two years older, he's still ok to play with most of the time. He never seems to get into trouble, either. A while later, they find their way back to their mom and dad. Their dad was preparing to put the clams on the hot coals. As he took the lid off the clams and poured them on the coals, it steamed and hissed. Quickly they covered the clams up completely with wet seaweed. Everyone cheered and started snacking on the food. The mood was light and friendly.

Stacy hoped he could be good and not make his dad mad. He wanted to enjoy the festivities. He vowed he would not speak unless spoken to. It was the easiest way to stay out of trouble. They already educated him with mealtime lessons, a squeeze to the neck, or a hand smacked across his back to sit up straight, or even standing while eating if you squirmed. He sat while his older brothers played with the sparklers. Stacy wore a pair of hand-me-down shorts of his brothers. They were too short and too tight; red, white and blue. He was uncomfortable with them. He squirmed like he had ants in his pants when his mom turned to look at him.

"Go, put some pajama bottoms on; you'll feel more comfortable.". He nodded, got up, and ran to the house before she could change her mind. Alone, he felt like he could stop holding his breath. Once changed, Stacy took the sharks teeth he found earlier and put it with his seashell, then he threw his swimsuit in the laundry chute. He wondered what it would be like to slide down the dark hole but knew it wouldn't be a soft landing.

He ran back to the beach. He was famished and wanted food. Stacy took some crackers and cheese and shoved them into his mouth. Remembering his manors, he looked around and realized his stepdad hadn't seen him. Slowing down, he properly ate one cracker and one piece of cheese at a time, taking bites, not putting the entire cracker in his mouth. Taking a sip of his water, he sat down on the blanket and was fast asleep in no time. Waking him, Victoria handed him a plate with clam's, potato salad, a vegetable medley and some clam chowder soup on it. He carefully laid the plate on the blanket in front of him and picked up his cup of soup to taste it. The soap burned his tongue, but he savored the taste.

He enjoyed all the seafood they got this summer and wondered if they would eat more at home when they got back. His mom was an excellent cook, but she made them eat mushy vegetables she boiled to death. That was the only thing Stacy gagged over; they were mushy and tasteless. Hard for him to swallow. They still made him to sit until he ate it all. Down the beach, as far as they could see, people had started their bonfires. They were so huge it was like everyone tried to make theirs the biggest. He looked around in amazement as the fireworks went off over the water; it was so pretty. He wished they would let him go sit on the rocks. Continuing to eat while watching the fireworks and looking at all the bonfires, he saw a firefly and became excited.

"Mom, Mom, look at the firefly," Stacy said while pulling at her sleeve. She smacked his hand away.

"Look what you've done. You made me spill some of my soup." Shrinking at every word, he wished he was invisible again and left alone. The summer went by quickly. The Haas family's daily life fell into a routine at the beach. There were a lot of power struggles to go on with Robby and their dad lately. Stacy learned to become invisible in plain sight, and when he was not, he almost always got into trouble. Today would be no different. While he sat on the porch waiting on Lindsey to get there, Stacy spilled his juice and his dad yelled at him. He sent him to his room, and he once again wondered when and if he will ever get his Star Wars figures back. He heard Lindsey and the others downstairs, but his dad had already told him he was not to come back down until tomorrow morning. Slowly he climbed into his bed; he felt broken like the shark's teeth he found today and cried himself to sleep one more night. He had dreamed again, but this time it was not about New Zealand, it was about floating away. Becoming invisible to everyone that was called family to him.

He was happy he still had Lindsey. Stacy knew she was the only person who treated him kindly.

FIVE

STACY WAS NOW SEVEN YEARS OLD AND IN THE THIRD GRADE.

He still enjoyed as much time away from home as possible. His anxiety level was at a whole new level. Just the thought of having to go home put him in a tailspin. He gradually learned what rules to follow and the consequences of not following the rules. What bothered him was when he got punished. He knew what he was being punished for. What he didn't know was why he was never told how to do it properly, or why certain things he did were wrong. This made it a tough lesson and a long road to self-discovery on what Albert and Victoria considered proper. Being physically abused only left him more confused and hurt. He learned to make his bed each morning and folded his clothes and put them away. In Alberts world, it had to be nothing less than perfect. He had learned that the hard way over the last two years.

Stacy was not looking forward to today. He had to wear this uncomfortable and stiff suit. He squirmed in the mirror as he attached the snap on tie, as he called it. He felt well out of his element and wondered where his clothes were that he wore in New Zealand not so long ago. He complained to his dad.

"Dad, do I have to wear this suit?" Albert looked down at him.

"Yes, you do. I'm getting married today. If you want to attend the wedding, you'll wear the suit." Frustrated and angry, Stacy stormed off to his room. He started hitting his head on the wall when Albert entered.

"You want me to give you something to cry about?" By now, Stacy had become more defiant and started hurting himself when angry.

"Whatever, you can't hurt me anymore. I already did it for you." Blood ran down his forehead and threatened to ruin his suit. Victoria raced in and quickly ran to the bathroom to get some tissue. She returned and vigorously, she wiped the blood away. Stacy winced in pain, closed his eyes, and let out an "OUCH." Luckily, there were no more fights along the way to the church.

The church was beautiful, a grand old Methodist Church with high ceilings. Beautifully crafted pews sat in proper rows. There was an exquisitely made white runner for the aisle. The flowers lining the pews at the front of the church were pale pink and white roses, including ribbon and burlap. They cascaded down the pew and matched Victoria's bouquet. In less than an hour, she would be Mrs. Victoria Haas. Her nerves were on edge. Ready to fall like a kid walking along the edge of a pool. She wore her hair up with little ringlets hanging down her nape. Her dress was a princess dress with a high neck of lace, showing just enough cleavage as the lace turned to silk. It fit perfectly in all the right places and flowed like a sweet summer breeze. She wore a simple pearl necklace and earrings from her gramme, a handkerchief from her grandpa, for something old. A traditional blue garter and the softest pink lipstick finished the look. As Victoria looked in the mirror, her nerves settled down. *She became excited. Yes, this is going to happen,* she thought.

Albert, along with the best man, were chatting with the officiant. "So, Albert. You ready for this?" asked the officiant that was doing the ceremony. Albert looked a little like a wild animal looking for an escape route. He wore a black tuxedo, with a pale pink cummerbund.

He wore his dad's cuff links. He looked like someone that just left the Oscars, excluding the wild animal look all over his face.

"Yes, I'm sure." This was Alberts second marriage, but this one felt much different. Victoria was a strong woman. The type of woman he had known all his life, but with money, lots of it. The only kicker was all those damn kids. While waiting, he thought of the them. Victoria was still young. He knew she wanted a family of their own. He hoped Stacy would behave during the ceremony and prayed that Robby would show up clean. He was confused about where Robby's sudden defiance came from. He thought their mother spoiled them too much. A problem he'd solve. Albert smiled at Brad, his brother-in-law and best man.

"It's getting close. Do you have the rings?" Brad laughed.

"Relax, man. I've got it covered." Albert smiled and relaxed.

Then the organ played. As the last of the guests arrived, the organ sounded out in soft traditional melody. The music suggested to everyone it was time to begin. The crowd quieted in anticipation of the bride's entrance. The wedding party was a small one; a best man and a maid of honor. Victoria's best friend, Lindsey, was the maid of honor. She found her spot on the other side of the groom and best man. The traditional wedding march, "Here comes the bride," started up, and the guests stood. They watched the back of the room in antic- ipation of her appearance.

Victoria appeared in the open doorway, and everyone went silent. Older guests put their hands to their mouths in awe, and the younger ones cooed and awed. Victoria looked beautiful as she stood there beside her dad. They linked arms and began their journey down the aisle. She wore a shy smile; she looked like a little girl living out a fairy tale. Victoria stopped and kissed the boys and her mom. She whispered,

"Thank you." She was proud of how good the boys looked and their behavior. As they arrived at the altar, the officiant asked,

"Who gives this lovely bride away today?"

"Her mother and I do," Jim answered, kissed Victoria, and put her hand in Albert's. He took a seat beside his wife with tears in his eyes. Not too long ago, Jim didn't like Albert at all. He thought his daughter could do better and that he was too old for her.

As The officiant said their vows, a tear slipped past Victoria's eye and onto her cheek. Albert, with such grace, wiped it away with his thumb. The guests cheered loud and clapped,

"You may now kiss the bride." Nearing the reception held at the country club where Albert sometimes hung out, the boys grew restless. Excited, they had arrived; the boys practically jumped from the car while it was still moving.

"If you boys do not tone it down, you will not stay here," Albert said under his breath.

They nodded as she turned and walked away. Now red faced, he grabbed Victoria and whispered in her ear. Her cheeks reddened and felt the walls closing in. Shaking, she walked away. Going to the powder room, she picked up a glass of champagne off a tray being walked around by one of the wait staff. Taking a long swig of it, she felt it wash over her in the relaxing way she knew it would. In the powder room, she checked her makeup and hair, ran her hands down the front of her stylish dress. Becoming calm, she proceeded to the bride's table and joined the rest of the wedding party. Victoria looked over at Albert with a knowing look. No one knew what he had said to her at that moment to upset her so much

A few close friends made toasts. Then grampie made a toast. This toast touched everyone's heart. Most of the guests fought back tears. He held up his glass.

"To my beautiful daughter, I wish you the happiness of a lifetime. Strength to always be present, patience to be a wonderful mother, loyalty to be a good wife. To my new son-in-law. May you protect your family. May you love them. Have the strength to know when to walk away. Know when to stay and fight, and never go to bed angry. To you both, I hope you grow together and have a love that will crash any storms, climb any mountains and endure any roadblocks that come your way." Everyone clapped, a few wiped away their tears, and the band played.

A few weeks later, Stacy was still trying to escape the grips of his stepdad. He would hide, play by himself, or climb trees. One day, he climbed the tree that hung over the driveway. The tree was gigantic and stood approximately 40 feet high. Once he got to the top, Stacy could see over the houses. Startled, he tugged at his pants, and discovered he'd gotten stuck. The branch caught his belt loop. Frantic now with fear, tears nearly escaped his eyes. Stacy yelled.

"Help, Mom, I'm stuck." Victoria heard him calling her name and went outside; looking around, she could not see him anywhere.

"Mom, I'm up here. Help, my pants are stuck," She looked up and her heart fell to her feet as she paled.

"Stacy, get down from there right now before you fall." Stacy tried to wiggle his way loose as Victoria tried to determine if she needed to call the fire department. Like a scared cat, shaking, Stacy finally wiggled his way loose and started climbing down the tree. Once he was on the ground safely, Victoria grabbed him by his shaking arm and shoved him, nose first, into a corner in the living room.

"I dare you to move; you'll stand still with your nose in this corner for twenty minutes. Do you understand me?" she asked.

Stacy shook his head softly and stood there for what felt like an hour. His feet ached as if he'd run a marathon; they were burning from lack of movement. Stacy was not looking forward to Marco Island this year, more than any other time. When he approached his dad, looking as if he'd lost his best friend, he asked,

"Dad, do I have to go on vacation this year?" Albert looked at him with a tight jaw and furrowed brows,

"Stacy, you know that's not an option. Yes, you will go." Sulking even more as Stacy left, his head hung low completely defeated. The realization that he had made the National All Stars Baseball team that year, with the fact that he will have to pass up the opportunity because of the beach, was all too much for him to swallow. He felt as if there was a huge gumball stuck in his throat, finding it hard to breathe.

When they arrived at the beach, they stayed in the same house as previous years; their routine kicked in. The kids helped unload the car and unpack for their summer stay. Itching to hit the sand and water, they did a rushed job of their duties. Clothes hung out of some drawers, toys were next to the beds they would sleep in this summer, and the refrigerator was ajar. Albert took one look around and summoned them all to the living room pronto. Donald was front and center, always going above and beyond to please him. He looked at all of them, and with venom dripping like a snake ready to strike, he asked,

"Who didn't properly do their arrival duties?" The boys fidgeted as they stood there; no one spoke. "Donald, get over here," as Donald did as he was told, he grabbed him by the hair. Quicker than a bomb could go off, he smacked Stacy on the head, bringing tears to his eyes as he held his head. Robby, defiant as usual, stood there with as much venom as Albert had. All the boys were grounded for the first day, there would be no playing, and they had to redo everything the proper way.

"I want you to pack and then unpack everything the proper way! Why do you guys make me do this? What I ask of you is simple, yet you screw it up. Now look at me, I'm screaming, it's all your faults." Albert spat blame out while he was screaming so loud Stacy was sure the patrons at Sweet Annie's Ice Cream could hear him a mile away. Victoria walked in and wondered why the boys weren't out playing. Albert filled her in on how they'd caused him, once again, to lose control.

That evening, they had to eat dinner in the kitchen alone. The boys didn't speak to each other; they all held in their anger, hurt and confusion. Stacy had come to his own realization. If Donald gets in trouble for trying so hard to do the right thing, then why try at all. He decided if he didn't want to do something, or if he did what he asked and it wasn't right, he would get in trouble. The point to him was, if

I'm going to get in trouble either way, why do something he didn't want to do in the first place. The results were the same.

The summer at beach went on like clockwork. The boys met up with the full-time residence and neighbors they'd met the year before. All of them walked to West Collier Blvd Bridge, a place where some fished, and the older kids would jump off the bridge into the water. This afternoon it was low tide, and being a year older, the boys all wanted to try it. The bridge was high and the water low; it was scary but also offered some invigoration amongst the boys. Stacy held his breath and climbed up on the bridge's ledge.

"Here I go," he shouted, with a proud smile on his face. Feeling brave, he took the leap, and down he spiraled like a rock being thrown. He made a big splash as his little body hit the water. Swimming back to the surface to catch his breath, he cut his knee on a barnacle.

"You cut yourself," Robby said as he climbed the wall back to the top of the bridge. Stacy looked and shrugged.

"Man, that was outstanding," he glowed at the others. That day, they all took turns jumping off the bridge. Other days, the boys would walk the beach for about a mile to the Sweet Annie's Ice Cream; they'd buy slush puppies and candy cigarettes. The store was a quaint little establishment with thin wooden plank floors you could almost see through. It was a fun place to hang out; the old man that ran the place was always welcoming to anyone that came in. Usually, when they went to there, they'd walk to Sami's; a takeout only restaurant that served clam strips, fish, and chips and burgers.

"Robby, I want fish and chips this time," Stacy said.

"Ok, buddy, let's go order and we can sit at the picnic tables and eat." They ordered their food and sat to watch the traffic and other vacationers enjoy the afternoon. Stacy sometimes wondered why his family was so different from everyone else's. He would see parents laughing and joining their kids for ice cream or playing on the beach. He yearned for that, but knew it would never come to fruition with his family. The summer went on with visits from Albert's parents; they usually came down on the weekends.

"You guys make yourself scarce," Victoria warned, when those weekends came about. By the time his parents would leave, even she was afraid of his angry mood. He would yell at everything and everyone, slam things around; it took a whole two days for him to regain his semi-normal after their visits. At dinner, he grabbed Stacy's hand. Pulled it hard while twisting it.

"We do not hold our forks like that. If you cannot eat properly and use your manners, then leave this table now." Stacy blinking rapidly, trying to stop the tears from the sting of him pulling his fingers, shakes his head. He was done eating anyway, and this was the perfect opportunity to leave the table.

"I'll just put my plate in the sink and go to bed." Still weighing heavy on Stacy's heart was the fact that he was missing the All Stars. He could have played in other states, and maybe even go to the finals. This summer, like most others, he stayed to himself. He was still too young to stay out after dinner without his parents. Most nights he hung out in his room playing with his figures or his toy from New Zealand. Sometimes he would sneak and look out the window to watch the older kids play with the neighbor's kids. They'd play Frisbee, stickball, or football. He missed Shaun and playing a game of stickball with the neighborhood friends.

They had a gloriously mild day; the sun was bright, and the water sparkled. There was no humidity and a wonderful breeze. It was a perfect day to play on the beach. First, the boys made sandcastles together and carried buckets of water for them to have it circle the outside of their castles. Then they started horse playing; Robby slung some wet sand at Stacy and Donald. This turned into an all-out war of sand throwing. They laughed as the wet sand hit them; it was in their hair and all over their legs. Robby ended up with a mouth full; he spat, trying to get the sand out while the others stood and laughed at him. Their joy ended abruptly,

"Robby, get over here right now," Albert said. Robby jogged over to his dad, still trying to spit out the sand. He grabbed him by the arm and drug him inside.

"Put this in your mouth," he told him as he handed him a bar of soap. He looked at him with squinting eyes and took the soap.

"What happened? What did he want?" Stacy and Donald asked when Robby returned.

"He made me put soap in my mouth!" he told them.

"Yuck, eww, that's awful." They all spat on the ground as if they too had been made to put soap in their mouth.

"It's over now. Let's go in the water." Robby suggested. They ran and jumped the waves, rode them back in until their bellies were raw with scratches from pounding into the shells from being carried by the waves crashing into the shore. Lindsey showed up for Labor Day, a sign of summer's end. They had the clambake, watched fireworks and bet on which neighbors' bonfire was the largest this year.

SIX

STACY WAS NOW EIGHT YEARS OLD AND IN THE FOURTH GRADE.

B y now, he escaped to a secret hiding place. He came across a cabinet in the hall closet that had a hole in the back of it where it attached to the wall. It was a small hole, but he knew he could fit through. He climbed through with a flashlight and ended up in the eaves of the roof. Knowing no one could find him there, this spot became his. He still played baseball and hung out with Shaun most of the time. His mom was pregnant, and all she did was get meaner and cross-stitched for the new baby.

"Mom, can we get a dog, please?" Stacy asked one evening. Looking up, Albert looked at Victoria to see what her expression was. Working on a cross-stitch of her new baby boy's name to put over the crib, she looked up. Shrugged her shoulders and returned to the cross-stitch. They had named their son Conrad. He took up most of their stepmom's time, and for this, Stacy was happy.

"I don't see why not? I'll look around and see what's available." Albert answered for his mom. Two days later, he brought home a German Shepherd puppy. Stacy played with the puppy all the time. He wanted to sleep with him, but Albert put his foot down. The dog had to sleep in a crate. Sometimes Stacy would crawl in there with him before he would go to bed. Sleepily, Stacy went to his room and jumped into his bed. Now that there was another person in the house and his oldest brother had moved out, Stacy shared an attic bedroom with Donald. It was a large space that didn't have air conditioning or heat. In the winter, it was comfortable, but in the summer, it was brutal. There were two large windows that were hard to open, that offered little in a way of a breeze. Still afraid of the boogeyman, Stacy jumped five feet to his bed and landed hard on his mattress. The bed squeaked from the blunt force. Donald waited until Stacy was comfortable and started his thirty-minute journey crawling across their floor like a snail.

Trying not to make a sound, he finally reached Stacy's bed. He reached his hand up, grabbed Stacy by the leg.

"Boo," Donald yelled. As white as Casper the Ghost, Stacy jumped up and screamed. He leaned over the bed when he heard Donald laughing and punched him in the face. Knowing if it bruised in the morning, he would be in big trouble. It worried him enough that he could not fall asleep that night. An hour passed when Stacy got up and got a jawbreaker. He loved them and enjoyed this one's sweetness. Albert came up the steps to check on them, thinking he'd heard something.

"What are you eating? A jawbreaker." Putting his hand out,

"Give it to me." Stacy handed him the wet jawbreaker. Albert then shoved it in his mouth hard and held his mouth shut. Stacy felt his teeth chatter and wondered if he'd broken any with all the force he'd used. Tears stung his eyes. He tried to get him to stop rocking his head. Finally, he released him and stared down at him.

"Never eat unless you ask first. Understood."

He shook his head and turned his back towards him to face the wall as the tears fell like a waterfall. The next morning, Stacy headed out to Shaun's on his bike to go to their baseball game. He wore cleats, socks and baseball pants that were hand-me-downs. His glove was so worn the threads were coming loose and stung when he caught the ball. The cleats were too small and hurt his feet. After two years of asking and not having his parents to come to a game, Stacy gave up asking. He always had other parents and his friends there. He enjoyed playing baseball and was good at it.

"Ok Stacy, you're up. Let's knock it out of the park." Shaun said.

"I got this." He approached the home plate. The first pitch was a ball, the second one a strike. On the third pitch, Stacy hit it far into the outfield.

As he ran the bases, all his teammates came up to the plate to greet him coming home.

He had hit a home run. Out of breath and smiling, he gave his teammates high five's and they retreated to the dugout. After they won their game, they rode their bikes to Stacy's house.

The boys played outside a bit.

"I got to go. Want to go to the park tomorrow?" Shaun said.

"Sure, I'll come by when I'm done with my chores."

"Man, your parents are mean."

"Yea, I know. Try living with them." Stacy ran to the door about the time Donald came out. Their German Shepard puppy escaped at that moment. Stacy ran after him and called his name as the puppy ran out onto the road. He saw the car, and a panic-stricken Stacy stopped dead in his tracks as the puppy got hit by the car. Crying, he walked to the gate and slammed it. Now his stepdad was at the door with his hands on his hips and a wooden bat in his hand.

"What just happened?" Stacy started hitting his head up against the brick wall.

"Stop that this minute. The neighbors will think you're crazy." Stacy looked up at him with anger and hatred in his eyes. Squinting his eyes at him, he could feel blood droplets as they ran down his forehead. He walked past his stepdad. Stacy went to the bathroom to clean himself up. He had been self-mutilating for a while now. He knew he wouldn't come after him when he got that angry. It was easier to punish himself than have him punish him for something he had no clue of what he had done. When his mom got home, they buried the puppy. His mom never asked Stacy what happened to his forehead. The next morning Stacy got up early. His head was sore. He skipped breakfast to go swim with Shaun. He walked over and jumped the fence. Shaun met him at the door. Going inside, Stacy smelled fresh cinnamon in the air and felt the warmth of home. He took in the scent with a deep breath. Suddenly he was hungry, and his stomach growled.

"Man, why do you keep doing that to yourself," Shaun asks. He referred to Stacy's forehead. Stacy shrugged.

"If I do it, he doesn't touch me. Basically, I do it to spite them."

"they are evil. But you have to stop hurting yourself." He said as his mom walked into the living room.

"Hi, Stacy. Would you like a cinnamon roll?"

"Sure." The boys followed her into the kitchen. As Stacy took a bite of the warm, soft roll, it melted in his mouth. The creamy icing danced down his chin. He wiped it off and enjoyed the rest of it. After both boys ate two rolls, they headed to Shaun's room.

Stacy fell asleep while Shaun played his video.

He dreamed of the time when Robby was about sixteen years old and was Stacy's idol. He occasionally took him to his baseball games and even watched. He promised to go to Stacy's game that afternoon, and Stacy was excited about that. He hadn't liked all the fighting Robby and Albert had done. Robby got in trouble a lot in those days. He drank and drove and once got caught with a joint in his car. Back then, a lot of teenagers drove before they got their license. Parents and the police turned a blind eye to that law. "Hey little man, good luck at the game today," Robby said. "Thanks. Are you still coming?" Robby shook his head yes, waved and went inside the house. Stacy woke up when he felt Shaun shaking him.

"You fell asleep. Do you still want to go swimming?"

"Of course." Stacy said and jumped off the bed. After swimming for a while, they went to walk in the woods. They came across a smoldering fire from the night before; the stoners had left it unattended. Swiftly, they found leaves and twigs to start the fire again.

Shaun and Stacy sat around and talked about Stacy's home life, girls and sports.

"Did you see Susie today! She's getting boobs; I saw her bra strap," Stacy said as he laughed at the notion. Shaun started laughing,

"That's funny. I'll have to look closer tomorrow. I kissed her once on a dare." He offered. Stacy turned red and looked at the ground.

"I've kissed no one yet, maybe this year." After a bit, they laughed harder as they peed on the fire to put it out and headed home. After he hung out with Shaun for the better part of the day, Stacy went home. When he walked through the door, Albert addressed him.

"It's time you get a job.". Stacy looked at him, rolled his eyes, and pulled at his hair.

"Ok, and just where would an eight-year-old get a job?" he asked.

"Get a paper route by tomorrow." Stacy walked off and went to talk to Donald.

"How do I get a paper route?" Donald looked over at him.

"Go to the office where they print the paper and ask for a route."

Stacy shook his head and hopped on his bike. Satisfied with his paper route, he smiled as he came through the door.

"I got a job. I start tomorrow." Albert looked at him with a shrug, as if he didn't care. Stacy got up early and started on his route. Carrying all the newspapers across his chest in a tote. He rode his bike and delivered all of them. The summers were the worst, it was so hot. By the time he was done with mowing, he was wet with sweat. He had to practice windsurfing, do homework, and get to basketball practice. Looking around, Stacy felt a stab to his heart; he missed his puppy a lot.

His stepdad did nothing but clean, feed them, and look after baby Conrad. If possible, he was even more evil now. By this time, Stacy raised himself. Still feeling lonely and displaced. He valued his friendships and the escape, along with all the support they gave him. The way Stacy described his dad's actions since Conrad was born was simple. He had his own kid now, and for the other boys, he was just a babysitter; he resented it and was sick of it. Thus, the reason they always got punished, yelled at and tortured. The anxiety of having to go home after school or playing was real. Stacy always wondered if he forgot to do something. Would he be punished at dinner with a wooden spoon, or a slap on his back or head, or worse. It was a lonely and scary place to be, his anxiety almost crippling at the thought of going home. This year Stacy didn't bother even being recommended for the All Stars team. After missing the first year he was chosen, he let the coaches know there would be no chance he could play for the All Stars.

Marco's Island was the best for him this year, even if he had to miss All Stars. The summer started out as usual, though none of the boys made the mistake of hurrying to finish the unpacking to go play. They did it right the first time, so they didn't repeat last year and not be able to go out at all on that first day. Stacy could go out after dinner if he was home by sunset. This year he was old enough to go to the Friday night dance at the pavilion there on the beach. Excited, he rushed through dinner without being noticed. Relieved, he asked if he could be excused. All the boys had planned to go to the dance. They washed up and wore their best shorts and t-shirts. When they walked up to the pavilion most of the girls were dancing. They were doing the bump to the disco song *Funky Town by Lipps Inc.* Stacy watched with his mouth half open as the girls swayed their hips and bumped sides with each other.

As the music changed to a slower song, one that Stacy couldn't remember. However, he remembered how it felt the first time to experience girls paying attention to him. A little red-headed, freckled faced girl walked right up to him.

"Want to dance?" he looked from side to side as if she must be talking to someone else. Then he looked at her,

"Sure." She led him to the dance floor, where he danced his first slow dance with a girl. That night was incredible; Stacy even got up enough courage to ask her on a date.

"Um, do you think, would you like to go to dinner at *Sami's*

Italian Restaurant for dinner tomorrow?" He held his breath and waited for the frog to leave his throat.

"Sure, I'll go. What time?" The little girl blushed.

"Let's meet at 5 o'clock." They agreed to meet in front of *Sami's* the next evening.

All day Stacy walked on air. He hummed to himself as he played and waited for the opportunity to tell his parents he had a date. Eying both under the umbrella, he figured there was no time like the present. He strolled over to where they sat, smiled.

"Mom, Dad, I have a date tomorrow. I'm taking Marybeth to dinner at 5 o'clock." They shook their heads ok and Stacy even saw his mom's lip curl up ever so slightly with a smile. Stacy showered and dressed; he wore his best shorts and a plaid button-down shirt. He walked the mile along the beach to reach his destination. He spied Marybeth and her father waiting outside for him. They exchanged pleasantries; Marybeth's dad asked if he should leave them some money.

"No Sir, I have the money. I earned it on my paper route. Thank you though." With a grin, the girl's father waved them on and went back to his vacation home. They entered the restaurant,

"Could we have a table for two, please?" Stacy asked the hostess. She gathered menus and walked them to a quaint two-person table near the window. Stacy held out the chair for Marybeth, then took his own seat. They ordered soda and looked over the menu. Stacy ended up with fish and chips, and Marybeth got a burger and fries. As they ate, they talked little; both were shy. The food was good. She thanked Stacy, and they held hands as he walked her home. Stacy had never felt so proud; he asked a girl out on a date. He arranged it and paid for it with no help from anyone. He walked home grinning from ear to ear; it was the brightest smile he'd ever worn.

The rest of the summer, they spent avoiding Albert and hung out with their summer friends. They played a lot of stickball, and every few days they would go jump off West Collier Blvd Bridge. One evening, Stacy saw Marybeth and her family sitting on the beach. He went over to her and said hi. They played for a while and took a short walk, holding her hand as they strolled the shore's edge. She pulled him off towards a dune, where she kissed him as the sun was setting. Feeling lightheaded, Stacy felt like he was floating away. His mind whirled around. He couldn't wait to tell Shaun about this summer and how perfect it was. The two of them chased each other and played at the water's edge for about an hour until it was time for them to go home.

Labor Day came and went with Lindsey's company. Stacy told her all about his first date ever. Everything was semi-normal, the first time Stacy felt, at least at the beach. If they didn't interrupt Albert, they didn't get punished as much. It was Labor Day, and the clam-bake was in full steam, literally, the steam twisted up in the air like smoke. The feeling and aroma of all the clambakes and bonfires made everyone feel festive. Getting ahead of himself, Stacy came tumbling down the steps, hitting his head against the railing on the way down. Hearing the thump, thump, thump of someone tumbling, Albert ran to the bottom of the steps, where Stacy landed inches from his feet. He had a small gash on his forehead, and his butt hurt from hitting every step on the way down. Albert's eyes looked like that of a raged bull, with flaring nostrils that Stacy feared might blow out fire. He quickly gained a little composure and got to his feet. He grabbed him by the arm, dragging him to the corner. He's yelling,

"What the hell, why is it you cannot do anything right! I demand you learn to control yourself. You are such a little hellion! Look what you've done!" All the while, he's hitting him on the legs with a wooden spoon he held in his hand. As he shoves him into a corner, he dares him to move. Standing there, Stacy could feel the blood slowly oozing from his forehead, running down the side of his face. He knew if he moved, he would be in more trouble, but he'd be in trouble if blood got on the wall as well. He ever so slowly and quietly put the collar of his shirt on his forehead to stop the bleeding. Stacy discov-ered most of the liquid was from his tears, not blood. Relieved he wasn't bleeding too much, he stood there the twenty minutes as he was told. After cleaning himself up and checking out his cut in the mirror, he joined the family and Lindsey on the deck. Nothing was mentioned or said about what had happened. They ate and enjoyed the fireworks; the boys all betting on which bonfire was the largest this year. Their summer ended once again.

SEVEN

STACY WAS NOW NINE YEARS OLD AND IN FIFTH GRADE.

T his year Stacy would be going to a new school. They had shut his previous school down over the summer for lack of kids. There were two elementary schools that would split the attendance from his current school. It would be his first time riding a school bus as well. They were bussed across town. There were a lot of fights that year. Kids from the center of town did not get along with kids from the east side, where Stacy was from. With the mix of kids, there was a division that scared Stacy. He often felt doom lingering in the air. Today was no different; he went to his dad,

"Dad, I'm worried and scared. The kids at school are always getting into fights." Albert looked at Stacy with little emotion.

"Get over it; toughen up. Don't let people push you around," he told him. Stacy started playing football that year and he began to bulk up. No matter how often he went to his parents, they never got involved. It was clear, it would be up to Stacy to defend himself or be as invisible as possible.

"Hey man, this is practice. You don't have to hit so hard," Aaron said, looking over at Stacy. The coach chuckled and said,

"Toughen up, Aaron." Stacy walked away with a smile. He liked football. It allowed him to hit people and not get in trouble. Football gave him a way to get out his anger and frustrations. Sore after practice, he headed for the bus. It was the weekend, and he was spending it at Shaun's. He was excited about the thought of spending the weekend free from arguing and abuse.

"Hey Stacy, let's get a snack and jump off the roof into the pool," Shaun said, running into the house. It was a warm day, and they decided a good day for a swim. Stacy followed Shaun to the kitchen, and they grabbed some brownies to eat. After changing into their swimming trunks, they headed for the roof. Shaun was the first one to jump off. It looked scary from way up there, and Stacy grew nervous.

"Woohoo. Man, that was fun! Jump Stacy." Shaun said as he yelled in excitement at the adrenaline rush. Stacy crept over to the edge and looked over. His knees were shaking, and he wondered if he had the nerve to do it. Then suddenly, he took a leap and was free falling in the air. It all happened so fast; it was less than a minute later when he hit the water. He sank to the bottom of the pool immediately, then bounced up to float with his head out of the water.

"You're right; that was a blast." The boys laughed and continued to play. They jumped a few more times. Stacy jumped, but he hit the lining, not hurting himself but ripping the lining. He became terrified to tell Shaun's parents when they got home. Approximately an hour later, Shaun's mom came in. Stacy wrenched his hands with a look of fear written on his face.

"Hi boys, how are you guys doing?" They quickly glanced at each other.

"Mom, we accidentally tore the lining in the pool."

"Let's go look," she said. The three of them walked out to the pool.

"I'm so sorry," Stacy said. Turning to look at the tear, then at Stacy.

"Honey, accidents happen. It is no big deal. We can fix this." She responded with laughter. Instantly Stacy was relieved, and they all laughed about it. The two boys kept the part of jumping off the roof to themselves. Later that evening, Shaun's dad repaired the lining as his mom cooked dinner on the grill.

"Dinners ready," she announced to the group. The boys got towels and started drying off.

"Stacy, let's eat out here, then we can go swimming again after." Stacy agreed with Shaun, so all of them ate outside beside the pool. Stacy always loved being there and often wished that his family were more like Shaun's.

The next day, while getting ready for bed, Stacy went to talk to his dad.

"Dad, I'm still scared of school. Last week, there was a huge fight. Three boys beat up this one kid, and he had to go in an ambulance to the hospital." Albert looked over at him.

"Stacy, you're in football. You are strong and will figure this out. You can't be scared all the time." Disappointed by the conversation, Stacy went to his room to sulk. He couldn't understand why his feelings didn't matter. He often wondered if he would even be missed if he left. Over the years, he learned how to keep to himself and be alone in plain sight. He preferred it this way unless he was at Shaun's. Tired, he yawned and settled into bed for a fitful night's sleep of bad dreams. The next morning, Stacy quickly ran through his routine. He was quiet making cereal, washed his bowl and headed out the door. There were a few minutes to spare, so he hung out with Shaun while they waited for the bus.

"I hate this school. It's not fair they closed ours down," Stacy said to Shaun.

"Yea, I know. It seems to get worse and worse. I can't wait until high school." They both shook their heads, knowing life would drag out too long. High school could not come quick enough. Once on the bus, they settled in for the trip to school. When they arrived, there were cop cars and an ambulance. The bus driver announced they would have to stay put until he got the green light to let them off the bus. All the kids anxiously looked with wide eyes as they peered out the window at the scene. No one was badly hurt, however; it put a hollow pit in the bottom of Stacy's stomach. Finally, after what seemed like hours, they were allowed off the bus. Stacy continued his day like he did every day. His back to the wall, and his eyes wide open. He never smiled in school, and he often wondered why no one bothered or picked on him. He found out one day over lunch. A kid that Stacy knew from football sat down at the empty table where Stacy sat.

"Hey bud, what's your deal?" the boy asked. Stacy looked around,

"What do you mean."

"Well, you have everyone scared to mess with you." Stacy processed that for a moment and again looked around.

"I don't know why you would say or think that."

"Listen, you don't smile; you don't laugh or joke around. You walk around with a chip on your shoulder. Like you are ready to attack. No one here knows you. They can't read you or figure out what would make you crack." Stacy thought about that, and for the first time, a slight grin touched his lips.

"I don't know man. I just keep to myself." Stacy said as he got up and walked away. Later that afternoon in science, Stacy told Shaun what his teammate had said. Shaun laughed,

"Well, you are a different person here than at my house." Stacy nodded,

"Yep, that's my protection shield. My stepdad taught me all too well how to shut down." After they finished their assignment, the bell rang. They gathered their things and headed to the bus.

"It's going to be a long year," Stacy said as they climbed on the bus.

"I know. We'll be excited come next summer." He agreed with Shaun. The ride home was uneventful, as usual. The kids were mostly from the same side of the tracks that Stacy and Shaun were. They knew most of them from the other school. Stacy hurried home to change for football practice.

"Stacy, what time will you be back?" Albert asked.

"I'm not sure. Probably around six." Albert was playing with Conrad on the floor. Victoria was pregnant with her second baby. Stacy glanced at them and headed to the door.

He rode his bike to the school on the other side of town in full uniform, holding his helmet.

As he rode along the path, he wondered what it would be like with another baby in the house. He was thankful the weather was unusually cool weather. After an hour and a half of practice, he headed back home on his bike. His legs ached as if he had just completed a marathon, and the pads he wore held his shoulders down like someone was pushing on them. He walked up to the door and opened it.

"Dinners ready. Go wash up," Victoria said to him as he closed the door. He went and changed as quickly as he could. Stacy sat up straight as an arrow as Albert threatened with the palm of his hand raised. As his face turned red, he felt like hitting him. With clenched teeth, he asked,

"Can you hand me the ketchup, please?" Donald handed him the ketchup and laughed. In Albert's eyes, Stacy could do nothing right. After all these years, he found a flaw every time. If it wasn't the way he held his fork, it was slouching. Nothing was good enough for him. After they ate, the older boys cleaned up the dishes and went their separate ways to do homework. Stacy decided he would go out and play. He'd had enough of school and homework. He went out the back to see if Shaun was around. He caught up with him and told him about the arrival of baby number two. He shared with Shaun how he felt they were just kids Albert babysat and was tired of doing so. Shaun listened as he always did, with little judgment. His only advice was to try to stay clean around him. Still handling his paper routes, baseball, and any other outdoor sports the neighborhood kids started up, Stacy kept away when possible. He feared home; it was the worst anxiety he'd ever experienced. The unknown that he would have to walk into day in and day out was overwhelming. Robby's presence was almost nonexistent; he hung out with his friends and was barely around since he'd moved out. When he came around after a few days out drinking, there were instant battles between him and Albert. To Stacy, this life was his normal, yet he knew there was much better and craved that other life.

This year at the beach would be much like the previous visits. Stacy begun to stress about it; he still yearned to play with the All Stars Team. He remembered last year; the date, the kiss, and smiles. Even in ugly times, some good would shine through if he let it. At this point, his parents did not force Robby to go to the beach, since he no longer lived there. He simply wasn't allowed in the house when they weren't home. Stacy was sad that Robby would not be there; he would miss his *James Dean*. Albert gathered all the items on the never-ending list to pack up for the beach. The boys stayed out of his way for good reason. His parents had just left, and he was making more noise, slamming things around than a train would if it came straight through the house. He was in a mood.

"Donald, Stacy, get down here," Albert yelled up the stairs. Both came running down the steps to where he stood.

"Yes Sir?" Donald said.

"I need you two to run to the little gas station and pick up the things on this list. Do not get anything else and do not linger; get back quickly." Taking the list and shaking their heads, the boys headed out.

"What's on the list?" Stacy asked.

"Paper products mostly; plates, plastic ware, stuff like that." Donald eyed the list and held the money he had given him tightly in his hand. Once at the store, they split up the list and each went searching for what was on their half. They paid for the items and felt like they might have taken a little too long, it was crowded, so they started to run home.

"Took you long enough," Albert snapped.

"Go pack your clothes; we'll load the car tonight in order to leave first thing in the morning." He brushed them away as he took the bags off their hands. They ran upstairs and started packing. Stacy grabbed his figures and his toy from New Zealand; he stilled played with both regularly. Tucking them into his suitcase, he thinks back to when his stepdad took his figurines. It had felt like forever until he got them back. He made a mental note not to have them out when he was angry. All packed, the boys descended the stairs and carried their bags to the car where their dad was loading it.

"Hi dad. Here are our suitcases," Stacy said.

"Ok, run along; I'll get them packed in the car. See if your mother needs any help. Scratch that, make yourself unseen; she's in a terrible mood again." The boys rolled their eyes, as if Albert knew what terrible was. However, they took the opportunity to play in the front yard with their kickball.

Dinner time came and went with a slight disturbance. Donald had dropped his fork, so Albert made him eat the rest of his meal with his butter knife only. He would smack the back of his head anytime he looked clumsy doing so or would drop the food he was serving to his mouth on the knife. Stacy often looked over at his mom, trying to see if there was any reaction to this behavior; there was none. He couldn't understand why his mom let this go on. Albert had eyes in the back of his head. He could be playing, feeding, or changing the babies and still reach out and smack the shit out of the back of your head faster than a fly could fly off when you tried to kill it.

Eventually, everyone finished their meal and could leave the table. Plates rinsed and put in the sink; Stacy went to take a shower. Tomorrow was going to be a long first day of their summer vacation.

Stacy thought, *A summer at the beach was better than a summer at home. He imagined what it would be like if they stayed at home. Albert would be hard to live with through an entire summer with no beach. At least there, he loosened his death grip on them.* It only took them a few hours to get to their summer home. They had been going there for so many years they knew the drill; who got which bedroom, and what they expected of them on the first day. Stacy got out of the car and grabbed anything within his reach to help in getting everything unloaded and up to the house. He worked diligently and error free, like a swift cat pacing his prey. He was proud of the fact he hadn't got smacked yet and continued to focus on the tasks at hand. It was only after they put everything away that he could run around the beach.

He met up with the neighbors and fell into a game of stickball. They played for hours, taking brief breaks to cool off in the water. One of the older kids ran off to play with another group that had shown up. Stacy wandered off to play on his rocks that he did so often. Albert was lying on the beach, soaking up the sun, and Victoria was planning the clambake, basking in sun next to him. After dinner, the kids played hide and seek. One of the older kids gathered them, and they headed out to the stone wall. He had a backpack on him, which he grabbed something from and handed the boys a bottle. The kid had taken some of his parent's wine coolers. This was the first time Stacy had ever had alcohol. He guzzled the sweet, fruity, dry wine cooler and instantly felt a buzz. Slowly, trying not to bring unwanted attention to himself, he went in the back way of the house and made his way to his bed. As he laid there, the bed was spinning wildly in circles. He choked back the urge to vomit and closed his eyes. He was asleep two minutes later.

Stacy woke the next morning with a dry mouth that felt like it was full of cotton and a headache. He brushed his teeth and headed to the kitchen and joined his family for breakfast.

"You don't look too good; are you feeling alright?" Victoria asked. Stacy shook his head.

"I have a headache." She nodded to the aspirin, so Stacy got up and grabbed two and swallowed them, followed by a drink of milk. He thought, *I hope the summer is this good, my first drink, but I hope I don't feel this bad.*

The beach seemed to be the place where Stacy had a lot of firsts. His first date, kiss, dance and now drink. Excited about what might unravel this summer, he smiled to himself and helped clean up the dishes. Most of the summer he spent with a family a few houses down. They invited him to go out on the boat; he even got to control the little handheld; three horsepower dingy. He had a blast with their kids. They fished, using drop lines, a fishing line with just bait on the end tossed into the water. They caught some fish under the dock and bottom feeders sometimes. The kid that took his parent's wine coolers always showed up with goodies. One time, he came out and had a backpack full of fireworks. They took turns setting them off, sometimes almost blowing their own hands off. Stacy learned you had to be quick when setting off fireworks. His favorite were the sparklers. He enjoyed looking at them as they burned down in his hand.

This year's clambake was especially exciting. Lindsey was coming a day early, and Stacy could not contain his happiness. He bubbled over like bubbles being blown off your hands as you played in a bubble bath. When she arrived, Stacy was the first one to meet her outside with a hug. They exchanged pleasantries, and he helped Lindsey with her overnight bag. After lunch was finished, they took a walk on the beach together.

"Stacy, how has it been going for you?" Lindsey asked. With a shrug, Stacy told her about the fireworks, the wine color, and fishing. He finished with the fact that he missed Robby and he was struggling with the punishments and anxiety he had. While Stacy bent down to pick up shells or rocks to throw in the water, she chose her words wisely. "I cannot say for sure why your father does what he does. I know God is with you, and you are a survivor. You've come a long way across the continent to be brought back to your mother. There are big things waiting for you, son." Stacy thought about this for a moment and grinned. He sure hoped there was something more than life right now waiting for him.

Labor Day eve had arrived. Lindsey and Stacy gathered seaweed while Donald got big rocks. Victoria stayed on the beach blanket with Corbin and Matt. She did little anything that summer except lay in the sun and give Corbin anything he wanted. When she shopped, she always got him a candy bar or a soda, whatever he asked for. Neither Donald nor Stacy got anything. Stacy recalls *the other night when Corbin was playing with his food and spilled his drink. He did not get punished; Victoria simply cleaned up the mess. Albert turned a blind eye. It still felt so unfair to Stacy.* Back to the present, Stacy helps his dad and Lindsey dig the deep hole in the sand. He was old enough this year that his dad let him pour the clams on the hot red coals. Donald wanted to put the seaweed over it. However, so did Corbin, and sure enough, even though he was younger than Stacy, he got to put the seaweed on the fire.

After the clambake, Donald and Stacy kept the tradition of betting on which bonfire was the biggest one that year. They watched the fireworks with all the neighborly "Ewwws and Awws" and clapping at the grand finale.

"Want to go climb on the rocks?" Stacy asked Donald. He looked at Stacy as if he was talking to an alien, a deer in the headlights look.

"No, I'm not doing that. We'll get hurt. Besides, it's getting dark, and you know dad doesn't like us that far out at dark." Stacy rolled his eyes and wandered over to the sand dunes. There he spied Marybeth and a few of her friends.

"Hi Stacy!" Marybeth sang out. Stacy blushed and said hi to her.

"Want to play hide and seek?" Stacy asked. All of them said yes and they did rock, paper, scissors to see who would "be it" first. Stacy lost, so he started counting after they set the boundaries of where they could hide.

"Olly, Olly, Oxon Free, here I come, ready or not," he yelled as he opened his eyes. He looked behind dunes, looked in the outdoor showers. He wandered over to the rocks he climbed on often and spotted Marybeth. She squealed when she saw him and started running for home base. He tagged her out, and it was her turn to count. They played several rounds before Stacy had to go in for the night. Wishing them a good night, he disappeared to the deck, where all the adults were sitting. Out of breath from running, he practically fell up the steps and looked clumsy almost falling on the deck.

"Stacy! For God's sake, have some manners!" Albert spat out. His face red with anger, with daggers for eyes, he followed him inside. He looked like a wild animal ready to attack.

Albert grabbed him by the arm and drug him up the steps to his room. He grabbed his belt and covered his mouth so he couldn't cry out as he left big welts on his backside. In pure pain, he tried to fight his way loose and even tried to bite him. Albert was relentless, like a dog that had been caged for too long and finally freed. He kept bringing the belt down hard. Stacy finally stopped fighting and grew limp; he released his mouth and walked away.

Trying to ignore the pain and catch his breath, Stacy thought, *I hate you! I hate this place. I want to run and be free. I wish you would die*; a million thoughts ran through his head as he drifted off to a night filled with nightmares. It was a restless sleep. He felt drugged when he woke the next morning and his backside was sore. The bathroom mirror confirmed he still wore the signs of a belt. He would have to wear a shirt today. With resolve not to be near him, he skipped breakfast and went down to the beach, unseen by anyone. Victoria delivered breakfast and took care of Corbin while the others carried the stuff to the beach. It was their last day there and then summer would come to an end. Stacy spent most of the day alone, playing on his rocks. He found a few pieces of shark's teeth he buried deep in his pockets. When it was time to go, he helped load the car and sat in silence the entire trip home. Stacy had not eaten that day, and his stomach was giving him a fit. He was hungry. He gave in at dinner time and ate a second helping. Getting through dinner unharmed, he ran over to Shaun's.

"We're back," he smiled at Shaun. They exchanged high fives and Stacy started telling him about the wine coolers, fireworks, and beatings. Shaun shook his head and lowered it when he told him about the last night at the beach. Stacy showed him where the belt marks were still just as visible as if it had only happened a little while ago.

"I missed ya brotha," Shaun said, then,

"We'll be sixth graders tomorrow. Top of our class." They both cheered. Later that evening, Robby showed up. Stacy was happy to see him. They talked a bit and then it was time for Stacy to go to bed.

EIGHT

STACY WAS NOW TEN YEARS OLD AND IN THE SIXTH GRADE.

O n the first day of school, Stacy found out he had a male teacher. It was the first time he had one. From that first day, he could tell the teacher was demanding. One day, Stacy picked on a kid in the gym. The student pointed at Stacy and yelled,

"Get out of the way." About that time, his teacher walked up,

"Who's he yelling at?" All the kid's fingers pointed to Stacy. The teacher turned red from anger as he turned to Stacy. Hunkering down as fear sunk in, Stacy thought he was going to get killed right there. Feeling like he had so many times at home, he sank down, and his gut ached with fear. As he backed up against the wall, his teacher gave him a good lashing. He was loud and harsh, all the classmates hearing. Stacy was afraid of his teacher for the rest of the year. The one thing Stacy did like about sixth grade was that his friend Brian got transferred to the school. They had been split up the year before, but they had known each other since kindergarten.

After school he had baseball, so he headed over to the fields dug out. At the game, Stacy saw Robby sitting in the stands and waved. Robby smiled. Stacy hit a home run, and the crowd cheered. They won the game on two runs. Stacy smiled; winded, he ran over to where Robby was smoking a cigarette.

"Good game, buddy." Robby gave him a high-five. Pride clearly showed on both boys' faces.

"Thanks," Stacy beamed.

"Want a ride home?"

"No, I'm going to hang out with Shaun."

"Ok, I'll see you around." Robby said. Stacy nodded and ran off to catch up with Shaun.

When he arrived home later for dinner, Stacy noticed Robby was putting his stuff in boxes.

"What are you doing with all your stuff?"

"I moved out; you know this. I'm just getting more stuff. My friends and I have a place here in Port Charlotte." Stacy's face looked shattered and sad. He still hated this place. Robby had made it a little better. He was Stacy's hero. Even though he knew Robby was out of the house, he felt he might change his mind, since most of his stuff was still there. The holidays were coming up. Stacy thought back to the last three Christmases. Every year Victoria would catch them coming downstairs with the blinding light of a 8mm movie camera.

"Oh, mom," the boys would say, as they covered their sleepy eyes with their hands to block out the bright light. Stacy observed all the gifts. He had noticed the differences between himself and his brothers, compared to the baby Albert had with Victoria. This was also the year she had their second son, Matt. He noted Victoria had also made a cross-stitch of his name for above the bed as well. What was more obvious was the fact that neither he nor his brothers got an embroidered name for above their beds. Robby was like *James Dean* to Stacy. He loved when he came to visit and knew he would be by today. Victoria went to the door after Robby knocked.

"Hello, come on in. The boys are all in the living room," she said. Robby nodded and followed her into the living room. There were presents being opened and wrapping paper everywhere. It looked like a tornado had hit.

"Boys! Pick the wrappers up and put them in the bag as you go," Albert said.

"Hi, Robby!" Stacy yelled as he ran over to him and greeted him with a high five.

"Hi, buddy. Merry Christmas." Stacy was smiling like a kid in a candy store. He walked back over to pick up his wrapping paper and started playing with his recent addition to the Star Wars collection he had. He received *Darth Vader, Princess Leia,* and another *Luke Skywalker,* along with a carrying case for them. Swiftly, he ran up to his room to collect all his other figurines to put them safely in his new carrying case. After Victoria settled baby Matt down with a bottle, she assisted Conrad in cleaning up his wrapping paper. With a knowing look, Robby glanced over at Stacy. A small shrug and a grin from Stacy assured him that Stacy saw the difference in treatment among them by Victoria and Albert. His mom and dad fought a lot this year. It seemed more intense as time went on.

"Go wash up; it's time for breakfast," Victoria said. The boys ran off with their presents in hand to drop them off in their rooms and washed their hands. The pancakes and bacon smelled mouthwatering, like IHOP. Stacy ran down the steps and picked his place at the table. He puffed out his chest in pride as he had beaten the others and didn't have to sit right beside his dad. After the food was brought out, Albert ended up sitting directly next to him, which made Stacy unhappy as he slumped his shoulders. He had assumed his mom would take the seat at the head of the table next to where he was sitting. Victoria, however, took the seat at the other end, near Robby. With an unsteady hand he reached for his milk, almost tumbling it over; he saved it from spilling but left a drop of milk on the table. Albert reached back and smacked him hard across the back of his head. Stacy grabbed his head and winced his eyes in pain.

"Jesus Christ, if he spilled the whole glass, you would have fucking killed him!" Victoria raged at Albert. Albert gave Victoria a look that said he might kill her if she raised his voice at him again and left the table. They all finished breakfast, and the older boys did the dishes while Conrad and Matt got to play with their things. At four, Conrad was starting volleyball. Stacy wasn't sure why Albert wanted both of his sons to play volleyball. It wasn't like anyone in either family played, but he was determined they would. Stacy ran outside to catch up with Shaun and play. He'd also learned if he was home by dinnertime, he didn't have to ask to go play; he wasn't missed. After their winter break, they all headed back to school, except for Conrad and baby Matt. Conrad had volleyball practice in a town, an hour and a half drive, so his parents would leave the house at 4 am to get him to practice. This left the others on their own for breakfast. Stacy was particularly happy about this. He knew how often he screwed up around Albert and would rather do it alone.

While waiting for the school bus to pick them up, the boys started playing pick-up football. They were ruthless and carefree. Stacy caught the ball but landed hard on the pebble laden blacktop. His arm was bleeding, yet he kept on playing, and threw the ball to another player. By the time he reached school, he was dirty and bloody, looking like one of the *Little Rascals* after playing ball. As he passed by classrooms, the teachers looked at him in disbelief and shook their heads. He didn't much care what anyone thought. Suddenly he bumped into a student while he was looking the other way. Almost knocking him down the other boy looks at him.

"I'm going to kick your ass," the student said.

"I don't have an ass," Stacy said. Everyone in the hall that heard the exchange started laughing. Stacy discovered if he made jokes about himself and laughed along with others, it was ok. He started turning his self-deprecation into joking; he became the class clown. More than once, the teacher had to call him out to settle down so the class could learn. Even though Stacy would take part in morning football at the bus stop or an after-school game of stickball, he still preferred being alone. On one gloomy afternoon, after having another fight with Victoria, he walked to the park. There was a little canal he liked to wade across on the rocks. The trees had lost all their leaves except for the pines and palms. The sky was gray, with ominous looking clouds. It was cold and windy for Florida. He picked up some sticks and examined them, then pitched them into the water. Stacy wanted to ask his mom why they went to all of Conrad's practices, but he was the only kid on his team that never had a parent there. He had thought about that a lot lately. The wind picked up and threatened to take him along with it; Stacy decided he should go home. It was an uneventful evening at the Hass Residence. Homework, dinner, dishes and bed. If you were lucky enough, you escaped any sort of corporal punishment.

Stacy joined his mom in the kitchen. He watched her put together a recipe for dinner with intensity, his eyes burning as he stared. "Mom, why do Conrad and Matt get treated so different from us? They get treats, when we're not allowed. They don't have to sit at the table until everyone is done with a meal. They're not even made to hold their forks right!" Stacy said. His little face looked shattered, like a piece of glass that was ready to crumble.

"That's just the way it is son, times change." Victoria responded. Not liking that answer, Stacy continued

"But what do you mean, times change? I'm not that much older than them, and I remember when I was four. It was different." Victoria shook her head and shrugged nonchalantly.

"Go play and worry about you." With that said, Stacy turned on his heals and marched out of the house. His arms crossed in front of his body, his face turning red as he hit the stone wall leading up to the house. When Stacy went back in the house, he could hear his mom and dad fighting; as usual, he found a safe place, either in the bedroom or in the attic. This time, he went to the bedroom. He had bought a *Nintendo* with his lawn mowing money. It was the only time he could spend any of it. His mother kept it in the bank and would not let him touch it except for this one purchase. He played *Mario Brothers* until the fighting stopped. Then he got ready for bed. The next morning, his hand hurt from hitting the wall. He swiftly got dressed and grabbed a piece of toast on his way out the door to catch the school bus.

It started raining, and through the intercom you could hear the principle say,

"Today we will be closing in two hours due to the weather conditions." All the student's cheered except for Stacy. This meant he'd have to be home with his stepdad longer than normal. With his head down, he made his way to his bus and climbed aboard. He sat next to the window and watched the falling rain, wishing he could dissolve like the droplets that hit the window. Winter turned into Spring, and Victoria was planning another summer at Marco Island. Stacy resented having to miss All Stars, as always. This year he gained a little more freedom and with that he realized the beach was where he became independent, and he enjoyed what summer at the beach was truly like. The summer visitors came for cookouts, boating, and dance night at the pavilion. Stacy grew to savor this independence and beach family atmosphere. The friends he made there; he called his "Summer family." There was a group of them that would fish, jump off *W. Collier bridge* and eat at *Sweet Annie's Ice Cream Parlor*. This year Stacy took some of his mother's wine coolers. She hadn't noticed they were gone. He had his second drink; he drank it much slower this time. They set off fireworks and went to the dances. Stacy became funny here as well, like in school. He imitated *Weird Al Yankovic, Dr. D.* and other comedians. He could make a crowd of strangers laugh out loud.

When Stacy learned Lindsey would not be joining them on Labor Day this year, he was devastated. He moped around for days. Like three rainy nights, he was all gloom and doom. He spent his days on the rocks alone. His evenings in his room alone. Finally, giving in to having a little bit of fun, he agreed to go to the Friday night dance at the pavilion with the neighborhood kids. As he showered and got dressed, he wondered if he'd see Marybeth again this year. Smiling, he ran down the steps and out the door. They all met at the rocks to walk to the pavilion together. Disco rang out into the night as they approached. Stacy started singing along in *a Weird Al* voice and everyone started howling and laughing. They grabbed a drink and looked around. The other boys immediately hit the dance floor; some of them could dance, others looked like they were getting a shock treatment as their bodies jerked around out of tune to the music. An old classic *Funky Town* came on; Stacy and the others joined everyone on the dance floor. Stacy did the running man, then the robot; he was having a good time. There were many laughs, and they grew sweaty from all the dancing. There was no sight of Marybeth, Stacy's disappointment.

"Hey, guys, let's go for a swim in the ocean," Stacy suggested. At first, they all looked at him as if he'd lost his mind. It was pitch dark outside. Reluctantly they agreed and left the dance. Once on the beach, the moon lit up the dark water. Stacy was the first one with his shirt off, plunging into the cool water, letting the waves carry him in. The others followed suit.

"That was awesome!" Stacy said. They all agreed and sank into the sand breathless. Stacy knew he was late getting in. He was able to sneak in undetected; thankful that Albert had already went to bed. The next morning, he started in over breakfast.

"What time did you get in last night Stacy?" he asked. Stacy shrugged,

"On time. I'm not sure, but I know I got here by curfew." He looked at him quizzically, unsure if he believed him.

"I was up until your curfew with Matt." He concentrated on his breakfast, without looking up,

"I'm sure I was on time." Leaving it alone, he went to feed Matt. Corbin was in a mood, much like his mother's, and refused to eat. After breakfast, Victoria gathered the laundry and loaded the washer. She discovered Stacy's shorts were wet and full of sand.

"Stacy, in the laundry room now." He appeared in the doorway.

"What?" he said. She smacked him in the face, then threw the shorts at him.

"Why are these full of sand and wet? You wore them to the dance, right? Did they dance on water?" Stacy almost laughed in her face, but something told him he should show restraint. She looked mean as a wild cat.

"We went to the dance, then we got into a fight with the neighbors water hose, horsing around," In a huff, she walked out of the laundry room; saved by Matt crying. Stacy thought, *well at least the brat is good for something, and he ran outside to play.* The laundry room incident must have been let go; Stacy never heard any more about it. The family set up for a day at the beach, as they always did. Albert sunbathed, his skin nearing the staged look of old leather. He fashioned a deep brown tan by now. Stacy and Donald never had sunscreen applied. They burned three times and peeled terribly each summer, then they had a deep tan like their moms.

Labor Day was right around the corner; Stacy couldn't wait for it to be over this year so he could go home and back to school. This year, although he had had pleasant moments, was not as fun without Lindsey or Robby. On their last night's stay, they judged bonfires, ate clams with all the sides they usually had. They watched the fireworks; a sign of summer's end. It was a bittersweet ending; Stacy played with the neighbor's kids and could go out on the boat to watch the fireworks from the water. His mom stepped in and said yes when Stacy asked, before Albert vetoed it. From the boat, it looked like it was raining different colors of light, a thousand shooting stars. After the fireworks, Stacy was directed. He must go straight home. He did so; he didn't want to push any buttons. He slept sound that night and dreamed of being home and hanging out with Shaun; he hoped he got to see Robby soon.

NINE

STACY WAS NOW ELEVEN YEARS OLD AND IN THE SEVENTH GRADE.

While Albert visited his parents, the boys stayed and played out back. It was a warm summer day and Stacy was enjoying the quiet breeze and listening to the birds. He had picked up another yard to mow add to his existing four lawns. Although he didn't get to keep any of the money, he knew one day he would get to control what he had made. After he finished his jobs, he went to the woods to ride his BMX bike he had gotten for Christmas this past year. He loved how it felt to fly over the bumps and hills; he felt free, like a bird. There was no one there to yell at him, hit him, or pull his hair. Though Stacy knew when his stepdad returned, he'd be in a foul mood. He was always the worst version of himself after a visit with his parents. Even Stacy's mom tried to stay out of reach upon his returns.

Funny thing is, Stacy also knew, or realized, he would never take it out on Conrad or Matt; they never had to have table manners, never got the wooden spoon, or so much as a timeout. It was truly unfair how he was treated compared to his siblings. His humor never worked at home as it did in school. He had no such luck there, and his punishment was usually worse if he tried humor. Today was no different. Albert was in a worse mood, if that was possible. He picked fights with everyone.

"Well, I'm going to clean the kitchen," Victoria said.

"You do that; God knows you do nothing else around here," Albert snapped back. She shook her head and walked out; she knew when to pick her battles. He was mean as a snake today. Stacy instinctively stayed in the bedroom, playing his *Nintendo* games. After an uneventful dinner, Stacy listened to his music using a headset. Music was another escape for him. He enjoyed the undiscovered songs on albums such as *ACDC* and *Ozzie Osbourne*. He had collected an impressive amount of cassette tapes until CDs came along.

School was a challenge for him this year. He was in middle school now and his grades started to gradually slip. He walked approximately four miles to and from school. He couldn't take his bike because he had to cross a canal by walking on a tree that laid across it. His route was a physical work out, he had to go up a giant hill at a golf course, cross over I75, and through some National Tree reservations, just to reach school and home. He had witnessed a lot of fights and been in a few himself behind the dumpsters at school. Stacy had no interest in girls like his friends did. He liked riding his *BMX* bike, listening to music and Baseball. He was an All Star that year. The more he got into sports the more his grades slipped. He was now an offensive lineman for the school's football team, on the windsurfing team and had his lawn business, and played baseball. As a matter of fact, Stacy was the first person to play on the football team and play on the windsurfing team.

He did get to go camping with some older this year. They went to *Myakka River State Park.*

"I dare you to jump in the water," Stacy said to the other two boys.

"Nah man, you crazy? That water can't be infested with gators." Stacy laughed and started to take his boots off. The other boys couldn't believe it, but they started to follow suit. All three boys jumped in the water in their underwear. Quickly, like they had jumped in, they jumped out. Their lips blue and skin full of goose-bumps. Stacy wasn't sure he'd ever be warm again.

"Oh, that was cold!" Stacy laughed and said he'd had a blast doing it, though. The boys set up their tents and started gathering firewood before the sun set. All of them hovered around the warm fire and ate their canned beanie weenies for dinner. Stacy didn't sleep very well that night, he was chilled to the bone.

The next morning, they packed up and walked the river. They again put up their tents and gathered more firewood. Today they walked the trails and explored different trees, wildlife and nature. Back in the throes of homelife, he had become accustomed to the harsh words, punishment and lack of support. His parents had yet to go to a game to see him play or windsurf. His group of friends grew a lot this year, there were six of them that became insepara-ble. Stacy, Shaun, Steve, Larry, Bryant and Bubba, they were quite the group. Stacy spent most of his time at one of those guys' houses. They became his family, the ones that cheered him on, taught him, and supported him. He strived to be a better person and he wanted to be a little like each one of them. He also wanted them to be proud of him. Shaun was still his rock, his person, but each of the guys in different ways helped mold him to who he would become.

Steve was most likely to be class president. He was diplomatic, outgoing and charismatic. Larry was popular with the girls in school and had a killer smile; the girls giggled and said so. He was a good student with excellent grades. He came from a good family, with solid family values of respect, support and encouragement. Larry's parents were earth shatteringly different than Stacy's parents. Always warm hearted and welcoming Stacy in at the drop of a hat. Bryant was most likely to be class clown, like Stacy, he had a great sense of humor but could think on his feet. Stacy quiet often thought of the punch line after the fact. Bryant was also in the school band and played in a local band as a guitarist and singer. He was a talented singer and guitar player, they practiced often at Bryant's house. He and Stacy had a deep love for music, which connected them together.

Bubba was most likely to be class treasurer. The boy was a math whiz and an entrepreneur. He had more money than the others put together. He saved and made calculated purchases only. Him and Stacy liked playing *Nintendo* together; while trying to beat each other at a game, they'd grow loud and rowdy fast. Bubba's parents were divorced, and he lived with his mom. She was a nice lady, older than Stacy's mom, she was always pleased to see Stacy around.

Shaun was most likely to be class ringleader. It was him that got the guys together regularly. He would put on a sleep over, or his parents would have them all over for a barbeque. The three of them, him and his parents were entertainers; they allowed the boys to sneak sips of beer. They could sit on the rooftop of his house and look out at the night sky; they never got into mischief or trouble at Shaun's house. He was the cool one in the group, like *Fonzie* on *Happy Days*; there were no rainy days for Rich. Stacy walked home from Shaun's one evening after dinner. When he reached the door, he could hear his stepdad screaming.

"My Fucking son is nearly dead!" Albert spat into the phone. He had taken charge for Victoria who was too upset to handle it. The police had just left as he went through the door. Albert calmed down a bit and sat the boys down to talk.

"Robby has been in a car accident. He's in a coma and they're not sure he will pull out of it." Tears started streaming down Stacy's face.

"I was just talking to the insurance company. No one has started or completed an official investigation. They said Robby, and some friends were drinking and got T-boned, and the car he was driving flipped over several times. One of his friends that got ejected from the car is paralyzed." Shock settled in with Stacy. He grew pale and numbly walked to his room. Over the next two weeks, Albert went to where Robby worked and interviewed all the staff that worked that day. He wrote down names and license plates and finally got a settlement from Robby's insurance company. Robby laid in a coma for two weeks before waking up. He had brain damage, broken bones and a long road to recovery. He couldn't live alone since he needed help, so he went to live with his dad, George, and his sister, Elsie. Luckily, Elsie had joined the Army and was off to boot camp a week later. Robby was only seventeen years old and his life had almost ended. It took Stacy months to get over the tragic event. He coiled back into himself, reverting to be a loner. His friends reached out to him with worry. Finally, after he got to visit with Robby a few times, Stacy realized he was going to be ok. He couldn't remember a time he had been so scared.

After weeks of worry and being alone, it felt good to be back with his group of friends. They were having a sleepover at Bubba's house this weekend. In his excitement, Stacy forgot to shut the door all the way when he got in from school. He heard his stepdad slam the door shut and yelled at him

"Come here, immediately." Stacy stood in front of him. He was almost as tall as he was now. He spat the words out all over his face.

"Get in the corner and stand there for thirty minutes, now." Cussing under his breath, so he wouldn't be heard, he went to the corner. He came up behind him and smashed his nose deep into the wall.

"Ouch, you're hurting me," Stacy cried out.

"Then keep still, put your nose in the corner as far as it will go," Albert said, then walked away. Stacy counted to ten about a hundred times. It felt like, before he breathed normal again and controlled his temper. After time out was over, he ran upstairs and packed his overnight bag. He grabbed some of his *Nintendo* games and his *Star Wars* figures. Without pausing to say goodbye, he ran out the door, making sure this time it was shut tight. Once at Bubba's house, he relaxed and enjoyed the cookout with the others. The burgers smelled amazing as Stacy realized he was hungry. They played stickball in the backyard while Bubba's parents cheered them on. It was dusk when they gathered around the table to eat dinner. The mood was light and there were a lot of jokes flying around, as well as horseplay. They all helped clean up afterwards and then climbed up on to the roof to watch for shooting stars and listen to music. This was the type of night Stacy loved; no pressure, no mean people; just his friends, music, and the night sky.

As the holidays rolled around, even though Stacy had gained an amazing group of friends, this year proved to be the toughest on him. Almost daily, Albert had begun torturing him. His boys got away with more and more while he took the brunt of his anger. Today was no different. There was no school because of hurricane warnings, and he'd been bottled up in the house all day. For one reason or another, unknown to Stacy, Albert made him stay in. He walked on eggshells all day, waiting for the tongue lashing or a backhand across his face. He tried staying in his room, but he wouldn't have it.

"Stacy, get down here and play with your brothers. I need a break," Albert barked. Stacy took a deep breath, dropped his shoulders and wandered into the living room where the little shits were sitting there babbling.

"You need to play with them. You're not the only one here, you know. We let you come and go as you please. Well, that's over. You'll do your time with the family as well." Stacy plopped down on the floor beside Corbin and offered him some figurines to play with. Corbin started throwing them.

"I want to play volleyball," he screamed. Beside himself, Stacy looked down at the floor.

"Dad won't let us play volleyball in the house." This set off more of a tantrum from Corbin.

"God, can you just shut up," Stacy said under his breath. It was only a matter of minutes before Albert had him pinned to the wall. He was in rare form today. He spit in his face as he violently yelled at him, losing all control.

"You are a waste; you always make my skin crawl. I ask for one simple thing! Can you do that, NO you can't." He starts to kick him and loses his balance. Stacy thought about hitting him, but then thought better of it.

"Get in the corner and don't move. Thirty minutes. Here me!"
He turned around and stuck his nose deep in the corner. Later that
week, while his parents took the boys to volleyball practice, Stacy
climbed out the window and visited Shaun.

"Where have you been?" Shaun asked.

"My stepdad made me stay in and play with the little shits. Then
Corbin threw a fit and he made me stay home. I only got to sneak out
because they're at practice," He explained. School was out the rest of
the week.

"Mom, can I spend the night at Shaun's? He asked if I could."
Victoria looked at him with disdain.

"Not tonight, but if you can have some manners, then I'll let you
tomorrow night." With that response, he asked if he could go let
Shaun know. She agreed, and he ran out the back door.

"She said tomorrow night, is that ok?" Shaun said that was fine.

"Can you play a while?" Shaun then asked.

"No, bro, I better get home, especially if I want to come over
tomorrow." Shaun agreed, and they parted ways. That evening,
Victoria had a book club meeting, so it was just the kids and Albert
for dinner. Stacy stayed vigilant and offered to help. He was trying to
avoid any trouble so he could spend the night with Shaun the next
evening. He almost made it until right before bed. Albert had gotten
the boys to bed and Donald was already asleep. Stacy sat there
quietly, playing with his figurines. Not paying close attention, he
knocked over a picture on the tv stand. He swiftly and cautiously set
it upright, thankful it had not broken.

"Nice job! See, you can't even go a day without getting under my
skin." Albert said. Stacy looked down at his feet as he sat on the floor.
Like a bee spotting a flower, he grabbed him by the hair and drug him
to his room.

"Dad, please. I'm sorry," Stacy pleaded. With a whack, he felt his
face sting. He left the room without another word, slamming the door
behind him. Stacy only prayed the slamming door didn't wake up one
of her boys or he'd be in deep trouble. Listening, he didn't hear any

one stir, so he felt safe enough to let out the breath he had been holding.

The next morning, his anxiety was at an all new high. He could still feel the hand print she implanted on his face the night before. He rubbed the spot and got up, dressed and went to enter at his own risk, the breakfast table. Never knowing when the next punch would be thrown, or the nasty words be spoken.

"Good morning," he said to the table. They all nodded and said good morning. He sat and ate his breakfast in silence. He was too afraid to ask if he'd ruined his chances at a sleep over that evening. The cereal he ate seemed to curdle in his stomach like sour milk. To his surprise, Shaun knocked on the door an hour later. Victoria answered it and invited him in.

"Stacy, Shaun is here." She yelled up the steps. She continued her morning routine of tending to her boys.

"Hey man, what's up?" Stacy asked when he entered the room.

"We're going into Sarasota today and since you're spending the night, my parents wanted to see if you could come along?" Stacy's eyes widened. The question hung in the air.

"Go Stacy, get out of here," Victoria offered. In a flash, like an angry summer lightning storm, Stacy retraced his steps back to his bedroom, grabbed his overnight bag and the two of them left together, like a hurricane.

"God, I hate going to your house," Shaun said. Stacy laughed and agreed with him; Stacy, too, hated to go to his own house. Shaun's parents took them ice skating; then they had lunch in the city. They window shopped; Shaun's mother loved doing this. The boys ran ahead and goofed off. It was late afternoon when they returned to Shaun's house.

"Let's go play in the sand, build a sandcastle," Shaun said. Stacy agreed and they grabbed some buckets and went outside. After making a large circle they began to sculpt a series of castles. Shaun's dad had to come out and help them get the some of the taller pointed roofs of the castle's sculpted out. Then his mom took pictures, brought them an old straw flag of hers, some pebbles for the canal they'd built, and a small piece of driftwood for a draw bridge. They laughed as they decorated their castles, both deciding to leave it with no entry's. It was a funny looking sandcastle; they stood on either side while his mom took pictures. Covered in sand they began to feel scratchy and itchy, they jumped into the Gulf to clean off all they sand. After they dried off, they went inside and played a game of Risk. They talked late into the night, falling asleep in the wee hours of morning.

School started back up the following Monday. The holidays passed in a blur and the signs of spring were in the air. Stacy was looking forward to family beach time this year. It was the only place he didn't feel suffocated and trapped, after all.

"Mom, can we please take Shaun with us to the beach?" Stacy bravely asked one afternoon. With an evil laugh his stepdad responded.

"No way! Hell, I wouldn't take you boys if I didn't have to." Stacy walked away defeated, figured, shit, it was worth a shot. Stacy cussed more by the end of this year, mostly under his breath, and never in front of an adult. All his friends cussed when they were together. With spring, football ended, and baseball began. Stacy had become a local star and it disappointed everyone that he could never play with the All Stars team. This year would be no different. He was named MVP (Most valuable player) metal. It was a proud moment for him. Robby showed up for the ceremonies and cheered Stacy on as he received his MVP. After the final game, and all trophies were handed out, Robby gave Stacy a ride home. He dropped him off without going inside.

"See you later buddy." He said through the window.

"Bye, thanks for the ride, Robby," Stacy said as he backed away so his brother could drive off. In the coming days, the house was a whirl-wind of activities. They all had to pack, gather their normal list of things for the beach. Stacy was less than enthusiastic, though he tried to get into the spirit of things. So much had changed over the past couple of years. Lindsey and Robby no longer came to the beach. One thing that was steadfast was Albert's torturing of Donald and even worse was the torture he gave to Stacy.

"Donald, Stacy, breakfast is getting cold! You've got two minutes to get down here!" Victoria yelled up the stairs of their beach house. The vacations were always the same for Stacy. Like an undying tradition that started that first year and continued the following years; they had to search for shark's teeth each morning for Albert. The difference this year, Stacy thought, *Corbin and Matt were old enough to help.* To his dismay, however, their stepdad did not make them search for their mom's shark's teeth. No, this was only the chore for Stacy and Donald. They headed out the door immediately following breakfast to spend at least an hour in the scorching morning sun searching. The only good thing that came from this is solitude. Stacy enjoyed being alone. Rather, he preferred it. It had been a long winter; the ocean was refreshing. Stacy eyed Albert, putting out the chairs, blanket, and setting up the umbrella. He wondered *when his boys would be made to do anything.* After an hour of hunting for teeth; he had only twelve pieces to show for his work. It was not a small amount as far as sharks' teeth go, but Albert wouldn't be happy about it. "Here mom," Stacy said as he handed her his treasures.

"Is that all you could find? Maybe you should search somewhere else tomorrow. The rocks aren't producing much. At this rate, it will take your mom to the grave before the bowl is filled," Albert scolded. He shrugged,

"Can I go swimming now?" She shooed him away with the flip of her hand. For about two hours, he and Donald played in the water, riding the waves. About that time, the other vacation residents next door had arrived and joined them. They all sat on the same blanket while their mothers dished out their lunch bags. They ate, laughing and talking about their school year. An appropriate amount of time later, they could go off and play. Stacy headed to the pier to fish, while Donald stayed behind and entertained Corbin and Matt. Relived to be out of earshot or eyesight of stepdad and mom, Stacy dropped his line. A short while later, some of his summer friends showed up. As they caught up, they all fished. Growing bored with that, they decided to go bridge jumping. As the sun went behind clouds and the threatening clouds looked as if they would burst open, the boys figured they should head back closer to their homes. Along the walk back, they found a sea turtle stuck with plastic around his foot. The boys got the turtle untangled and let him go near the water's edge. Feeling proud, their chests sticking out, they stood tall as they returned and told their moms about it.

Though they didn't catch any fish, Stacy had a decent time catching up with the other kids. He couldn't help but wonder if Marybeth would be back this year. This always floated in the back of his mind when time to go to the beach.

"Stacy, I want you and Donald to watch the boys this evening. Your dad and I are going out." Stacy rolled his eyes. That only meant they couldn't go outside and play night ball with the others.

"Do we have to, mom?" Stacy said.

"Yes, your mother wants to go out," Albert replied. Bummed, Stacy went out on the deck to lie in the hammock. He listened to his headset. *ACDC* was playing; he closed his eyes and escaped with the music.

"Stacy! Wake up!" Albert said as he hit him in the head.

"Geez, you didn't have to do that." Stacy rubbed his head while taking his headphones off.

"We're leaving now. You need to go in and watch the boys. Do not let them get hurt, they're not allowed outside," Albert said and barked out more orders. When it was time for bed, Matt wouldn't stop crying and Corbin would not stay in his bed. Finally, at wit's end, Stacy told Corbin if he would stay in bed, he'd take him to *Sweet Annie's* tomorrow and get him some candy with his own money. This seemed to do the trick; Stacy just hoped his dad would let Corbin out of his sight for two minutes for him to do this. As for Matt, nothing worked. Stacy let him cry. About an hour later, his parents returned home. Albert was upset to find Matt with red, puffy eyes sniffing.

"Stacy, what the hell is going on. Why is Matt crying, and for how long? Look at him." Stacy neared the bedroom where his dad and Matt were.

"He wouldn't stop crying," Stacy said. He glared at him with dagger eyes.

"Then you should have rocked him." Stacy caught himself before he rolled his eyes at him.

"Dad, he's almost three," Stacy said.

"I know how old my son is," Albert screamed as he twisted Stacy's arm. Stacy backed out of arm's reach and turned to go to his room without a word. He knew he would get punished for this tomorrow.

"Stacy, you won't be going to the dance on Friday night," Albert announced at breakfast. Without so much as a word, Stacy ate quickly and went out to the beach. Albert spotted him on his precious rocks playing. He shook his head and started setting things up. Out of the corner of Stacy's eyes, he could see he was staring at him. He was glad he had not called him over. He jumped from rock to rock, found some shells, and then took a swim. He thought at one point he had seen Marybeth, but as the little girl got closer, he realized it wasn't her. Stacy was a little disappointed with that. Like every year, Stacy and Donald both got a bad sunburn. It hurt to put their shirts on their red-hot shoulders and back. Neither complained, however, because it would only mean more abuse.

There was only one other major incident that summer where Albert lost his shit, as Stacy had called it. He was cooking and Stacy was having an ice cream from Sweet Annie's. When he walked through the door, Albert stopped in his tracks.

"Young man, you aren't allowed to eat ice cream this close to dinner or anytime when the boys do not have one." Albert said, then took the ice cream and gave it to Corbin. Stacy stood there with a disbelieving look. His mouth hung open, his hand still in the air as if he was still holding his ice cream.

"I can't believe you did that," he said. With that, he slapped his mouth and made his lip bleed. He touched his lip and went to his room. They made him stay there the rest of the night without dinner. At this age, Stacy understood it was "their" punishment when Albert abused them. He understood his mom was aware of how he treated them and did nothing to stop him. He blamed them both, therefore it was their fault, not just his. Stacy remembered promising Corbin he'd take him to Sweet Annie's. He approached Victoria with hesitation. "Mom, can Corbin walk with me to Sweet Annie's? I told him last night, if you would let him, I'd take him and get him some candy." Victoria sat up and cupped her eyes from the bright sun. She glanced at Corbin, then back to Stacy.

"Yes, but if he gets even a scratch, you'll be in the house the rest of the summer," she warned.

"Ok." Stacy went and told Corbin to come with him. He took Corbin's hand and they walked the along the water's edge to the store. The cold air from the air conditioner that hummed overhead, hit them like a welcome splash of water. It was a hot day. Stacy got Corbin a cherry slushy and some gummy bears. Satisfied, Corbin tugged on Stacy's hand to let him know he was tired and wanted to go back. Stacy ended up having to carry him halfway back. He'd made sure Corbin was clean and ready to be handed over to his mom. Satisfied that he'd done as promised, Stacy ran off to play with the other kids.

"Hey man, you going to the dance tonight at the pavilion?" the neighbor kid asked.

"Yeah brotha, I'm going tonight; let's meet up at the rocks," Stacy answered. Later that evening a group of them met up at the rocks to walk over to the pavilion. Stacy had yet to see Marybeth. He wasn't that into girls, not as much as his friends were; they were girl crazy. Stacy would rather fish, ride his BMX, swim, or listen to music. He enjoyed roaming around the woods and finding cool things. He enjoyed being alone. Tonight, at the dance it was more his type of music, 80 rock ballads were played. They danced to some *Peter*

Frampton, K.C. and the Sunshine Band and Michael Jackson. The DJ played a good variety and the boys had a blast.

Stacy did the "sprinkler" dance, where you hold one foot in back of you with your hand and the other arm is stretched out in front of you and you bounce around in a circle, while pumping your foot; looking well, much like a sprinkler watering the grass. The boys got a kick out of this while trying to do it, too. After a few dances, they were all sweaty and thirsty.

"Man, I can't breathe I've laughed so hard. I'm thirsty, let's get out of here." One of the boys said. They all agreed and went over to the older kid's house. There, they each drank a beer. The kid's parents were out at a local party that night. Stacy checked out and headed home; he was beat and ready for bed. When he entered the side door, he noticed his parents were still up.

"Hi, I'm exhausted. Goodnight." They both nodded and said goodnight. Happy that there were no major questions or demands, Stacy slept like a rock that night.

Labor Day was only a few days away. With all the preparations well under way, most afternoons Victoria ran errands. Stacy immensely enjoyed this, because she took her boys along with her. In his free time from the three of them, he would explore. One afternoon he went under the bridge and watched others jump while he looked for little treasures. He found a rusted watch that no longer worked. On one afternoon excursion, he found himself near the pier; he walked to the end. It was deserted at the time and looked out over the horizon. He remembered how peaceful it had been. This peace he'd found evaporated as he walked through the doors of their vacation rental.

"Where have you been?" Victoria asked. Stacy looked at her and paled.

"I, um, went for a walk near the pier." She took a can she was holding in mid-air and flung it at him, cracking him square in the jaw. Stacy grabbed his jaw and ran out the door. About an hour after he'd left to walk on the beach and cool down, he returned. This time his stepdad was in the kitchen, making a drink.

"Stacy, what did you do to your jaw?" Albert asked, as he looked at it red and swollen.

Stacy's hand automatically moved to his face, where it was sore and hot to the touch.

"Why don't you ask her," He said and pointed to Victoria. He looked over at his wife, who didn't say a word, then continued making his drink and left the room. In disbelief, Stacy went to his room and laid on the bed. He couldn't comprehend why or how it came about that he got stuck with this family. He'd seen his friend's parents and often wondered why they were not normal like his family. After inquiring and observing, he realized it was his family that wasn't normal, not the other way around. Albert, Stacy and Donald prepped the sand pit for the clams; it was Labor Day Eve and there was a lighter spirt of anticipation in the air. The weather was crystal clear skies with a pristine beach and water that glistened under the rays of the sun. As the waves crashed against the shore, music and laughter could be heard. Busy bodies, locating seaweed, wood and stones could be heard. Once the clams were in the pit, covered and steaming, all that was left was to wait. They ate fancy cheeses and crackers, little necks, lobster rolls, and shrimp cocktail. There was enough food to feed a small army. Those passing by would yell out their hellos or wave as they strolled past. Stacy took a swim to cool off his skin; it was hot to touch from preparing the pit and the sun. As the bubbly water rolled up his calves, he jumped a wave and swam out. He wished he could swim to the other side of the world.

A while later, he looked back up the beach to where they had set up. He could barely make out someone in their group waving for him to come back to shore. Slow and steady, he made his way back and got out of the water, shaking his head to get the excess water out of his hair and off his face. As he approached the group, he could see Lindsey. With a huge grin, he went up and gave her a hug.

"Lindsey, I didn't think you were going to make it," he said.

"I hated missing last year, so my wife took off this year and we both came. Stacy looked over and shook Samantha's hand. Lindsey and Samantha had been married five years now. They were so much fun to be around. Lindsey, with her fire engine long red hair, tiny build, while different from Samantha's dark skin and curly hair. Stacy always loved being around them.

"Good to see you again," she said.

"Likewise, I'm glad you came," Stacy said. He and Lindsey took a short walk along the water's edge. They made small talk, and Stacy filled her in on what he'd been doing all summer. He enjoyed his time with her; she never pushed him to talk about anything he didn't want to. She simply listened and gave some solid advice. Later that night, like tradition, Donald and Stacy bet on who's fire was the largest that year. They laughed a bit, then Stacy went to meet up with his friends to watch the fireworks in the water.

"Bruh, wait up," Stacy yelled. Sam stopped and waited along with the other guys. They walked together to where the boat was docked and headed out to watch the sky light up with multi-color fire. This year's fireworks were the best so far, at least that's what Stacy told the group, and they had agreed. After the show, they went down to the rocks and drank a few beers that everyone had collected throughout the week from their parents. They stole them, their parents never seemed to have caught on. Feeling light and bubbly from the beer, Stacy strolled down the beach towards his home. For a split second, like the blink of an eye, all was calm and right in Stacy's world. He walked alone, which is what he preferred. There was no one harassing him, abusing him or pulling at him. It was a rare occasion that he could let go and feel free from the anxiety of having to return to his family.

As the lights to their house came into sight, the calm was swept away like the water that went back out to sea after crashing the shore. He caught himself, forming his hands in tight fists hanging on each side of his body. His only hope was that they would have already retired for the night. That was squashed about a second after he thought about it. As he got closer to the house, he could see them sitting on the deck. His head quickly dropped as did his shoulders, as he sunk into himself in a protective cocoon. He walked up the steps, nodded to them, "Goodnight."

They never said a word to acknowledge him, they were having a cocktail and talking.

They packed up bright and early after having breakfast. Once home, Stacy took off to visit Shaun.

"Hey brotha, glad you're back. How did the beach go?" Shaun asks.

"It went ok, had a few beers," Stacy said with a shy grin. Shaun gave him a high five, and they jumped in the pool for a while. They were mischief together, as they stuck the pool vacuum hose in the aerator and watched water blow out the other side. They splashed each other, dunked each other, jumped off the ladder into a cannon-ball. It was a carefree, fun afternoon. Growing hungry, Shaun's mom offered them a tuna sub. They both agreed and gobbled the subs down like a stray dog that found food. After lunch, they explored the woods across the way, like they did often. This time finding no smoldering fires.

TEN

STACY WAS NOW TWELVE YEARS OLD AND IN EIGHTH GRADE.

Rippled with dark gray rain clouds, the sky looked dangerous. It cast an eerie gloom through the trees in the woods. Stacy stood there, deep in thought, giving no attention to the pending storm. He remembered the scene as if it had just happened. Red faced and bulled up like a weightlifter on steroids, Stacy looked down at his stepdad. Pulling his arm back, shoulder level, he balled a fist and with pure hatred, he almost hit him. What stopped him was simple. He couldn't see hitting someone out of anger. He had more control over his anger than his stepdad did; he thought to himself. He had just kicked him, had lost his balance and as he fell, Albert had noticed the look on Stacy's face. He noticed his hand drawn back as he cowered down. He feared him at that moment. Stacy could see it in his eyes. He was scared. He looked at him and said, "You ever hit me again and I'll kick the shit out of you." Albert knew he was telling the truth. He believed him. He had never seen such fury in him. As anger overcome Stacy, he walked out the door.

That evening Shaun's mom called the Haas' to let them know Stacy was there, and not to worry. It was ok if he stayed a few days. Stacy did not return home for three days. There were two good things that came out of that battle. Victoria nor Albert never laid a hand or spoon on him again, and Stacy decided at that moment he would choose to be happy. He was tired of being miserable, tired of the self-mutilation, tired of the hate and anger. He could have easily gone down a different path. He wanted his life to be like that of his closest friends. He chose happiness. He depended on his friends for support, encouragement, and growth. It was also the year the boys ruled the school. Stacy played football and windsurfed again this year, as well as his lawn business, and baseball.

He grew to love sports, outdoors and being anywhere but home. It was an uplifting turn of perspective he had learned to cultivate in order to prosper instead of fail. When Stacy returned home the previous evening, nothing was said; it was like nothing had happened. Stacy looked up at the darkening sky and decided he should get home before the rain started. He took two steps and heard an earth-shattering roll of thunder and witnessed a streak of lightening ahead of him hit a large tree. The lightening did minor damage. Stacy quickened his steps, trying to avoid getting wet, hoping to beat the rain. With no luck, by the time he entered his house, he was soaked to the bone. He skipped every other step as he went to his room, undressed, dried, and put dry clothes on. He descended the stairs and observed the activity in the living room. Their boys were playing video games, he smirked; he was made to play his video games in his bedroom.

In the kitchen he could hear Victoria rustling around preparing dinner. His stepdad, no doubt, was in the shed, now trapped by the rain. *Lucky me*, Stacy thought.

"Stacy, set the table," Victoria barked. He nodded and went about setting the table. They spoke little these days, and that was ok with him. She or Albert would bark commands; he would do it or not. Most days he would comply, like with setting the table. That evening, Victoria demanded that Stacy sit at the table and eat his boiled squash before he could be excused.

"I don't like it. It tastes like bland runny paste," Stacy complained.

"Just eat the damn stuff," was her response as she walked away from the table and Stacy. He must have sat there for two hours before he pretended to eat it, but had been hiding some under his potato skin and spitting some out in his napkin. Finally, with an empty plate, Stacy hurried to the kitchen; scraping his plate to get rid of the potato skin in the trash and throwing his napkin away, he washed his plate and escaped to his bedroom. Little triggers like this happened frequently. Albert made up for no physical abuse by turning to verbal abuse or denying Stacy of things, while giving their boys everything they asked for. They were no shows at all of Stacy's games or windsurfing events as they continued to be dedicated to their boys' volleyball practices and games. One afternoon in the spring, it was beautiful outside; the perfect spring day. Stacy got an early start mowing lawns so he could enjoy the day. He had finished and retraced his steps back home before anyone had gotten up. He grabbed some cereal and decided he would go *BMX* riding on the trails in the woods afterwards. He peddled fast with experience and control of his bike. Hitting mounds just right to soar in the air before he smashed down to the earth with a thump. It was exhilarating. Now back on the street behind his house, he pulled up to Shaun's driveway and left black marks as he side slid to a stop on his bike. Shaun's dad was in the driveway washing the car.

"Good morning Stacy," he said.

"Good morning. Is Shaun inside?" Stacy looked over at the door.

"He is. Let yourself in." Stacy thanked him and jogged up to the door.

"Hello," Stacy sang out as he opened the door.

"Hey man," he heard Shaun say as he rounded the corner to the kitchen.

"Hey, your dad said to let myself in." Shaun shook his head and offered Stacy a croissant. He accepted it and took a bit of the buttery, warm bread that was so flaky it almost melted in his mouth.

"So, what are you up today?" Stacy asked after he had swallowed his food. Shaun chewed and then swallowed with a finger in the air to show one minute. After he swallowed, he said,

"I was thinking of going to the field to catch a pickup game of stickball." Stacy liked that idea and agreed.

They left the house a few moments later after letting the adults know where they'd be. The air was so clean, and the sun shined bright with a cooler breeze. The boys found some other neighborhood kids to play stickball.

After a few hours and several scrapes, scratches and cuts they ended the game, giving into hunger. They raced back to Shaun's house for some lunch. They talked about school, Stacy's mom and stepdad, the fact that next year they would be in the ninth grade. Stacy had told him about the settlement from the insurance company that went to Robby, and how much he had overcome in his recovery of the accident. He didn't mention the fact that Robby still had some brain injury that affected his thought process. In the back of Stacy's mind, he had hoped that it would get better over time. After lunch, Stacy told Shaun he had to go and thanked him for lunch as he took off on his bike. He loved hanging out there, but one thing remained true, he loved being alone the most. He enjoyed being alone, not having to think about others or if he'd do something wrong.

He went back into the woods and rode a while longer, then jumped off his bike to sit on a tree that had fallen some time ago. He played with the bark a bit and shuffled his feet in the dirt and browned leaves that laid on the soil. The earth smelled of fresh rain and was damp; he could feel his ass getting wet through his jeans where the rain had left the fallen tree wet. He had to go tomorrow to get a molar cut out and wasn't ashamed to admit, at least to himself, that he was scared. The next morning his mom carted him off to the dentist, who felt sorry for Stacy. His parents would not pay for the Novocain, gas, or any pain medicine; this was going to be a deal with it situation. Stacy couldn't help but to think, damn, they just want to torture me any way they can. He survived the pulling of his molar, medicine free, like a man. Even though it hurt like hell, he did not cry.

He exited the dentist's chair and went to the lobby with a large wad of gauze crammed in his mouth and one wrapped around his head. Victoria took pleasure in this. It was written all over her face. Stacy thought *she might as well laugh at my discomfort.* The next three days, his diet comprised ice chips, then jello or pudding, and finally soft hot food. It took a week before he could go back to school and start light activities. The rest of the school year went by without a hitch, and they had graduated to the ninth grade. Next year they would be high schoolers.

Stacy reflected on the past year; the triumphs, the fails, and all that had transpired with Albert. He thought about that dreadful day of confrontation when he almost hit him. Stacy thought things might change after that incident. To his utter disbelief, the only thing that changed was he no longer got physically abused. He still hated being there and would do anything to be out of the house. He still noticed the vast difference in treatment towards her boys and the rest of them. They got candy, gifts, and spoiled. They were not made to have manners at the table, much less anywhere else. There were no rules for them and no punishment of any kind.

Eventually, Stacy was told to find somewhere else to go during Marco Island beach family time. They no longer wanted him or Donald to go. They had to find somewhere to stay during the summer. Naturally, their boys went with their parents to the beach each summer. Stacy was only the slightest bit upset about this. It was a tad better at the beach than at home. However, it was still miserable being in the same house with Albert, regardless of if it was the beach. It felt like a lifetime ago since Stacy had been that four-year-old little boy starting his journey back to the states. He had learned the not so conventional way to behave to Albert's liking. He had long given up hope of reuniting with his biological father. In fact, he did not think of him much, nor saw him. On the off chance that he thought about the two families from which he came from, his thoughts were like a mouse trapped in the rafters trying to escape to freedom. He did not feel he belonged to any of them. Some might look at it as fortunate to have two families to choose from. Stacy looked at it as having two families and belonging to neither. Suspended in a world alone, left to figure it out and raise himself. Stacy belonged nowhere. It would be he who decided his fate. Him to create his path. Him to deal with the demons that haunted him with being and feeling so utterly "Invisible in plain sight." He became the lone wolf trudging through life, learning from observation instead of the guidance of a loving family. He was eventually comfortable in his own skin. It would take him years, if ever, for him to overcome the cruelty he had endured. He would have to face life's crises alone. He would have to build his own family to feel part of a family.

The End

30 YEARS LATER

Though Stacy finally escaped his family when he turned 17 years old to go to college. He discovered after several wonderful years with his college friends, road trips, ski trips to Canada, etc., he could not outrun his past. After a broken marriage, he returned to feeling worthless and to some self–deprecating habits. While living with a coworker, Stacy continued to support his family, leaving him with very little. He often wondered why the old wounds would flare up, even though he tried to keep the walls he had built so many years ago strong. Some days he would find the joy of life, as it would seep through, like seeing a dolphin jumping in the water as he drove his truck for delivery. His passion for and admiration of the little thing's life gave him ran deep.

After regaining the frame of mind that Stacy had so many years ago in college, Stacy began to live again. This is when Isabelle came into this life. He looked at her and smiled, "You look so cute." Shy, Isabelle could feel her face flush as she hid a slow smile.

"You should probably keep your eyes on the road," Isabelle suggested. Stacy laughed and as he focused on the road again, memories of his past flooded in. He recalled the first time he had met

Isabelle; she was broken, insecure, abused and almost homeless. She was the most beautiful woman Stacy had ever met. As he got to know her, his heart ached at the abuse she had endured through her journey of life. Feelings swept over him as he reached over and turned up the air conditioner his body grew warm in the car. He was ashamed that he ever complained about his upbringing, feeling it paled compared to Isabelle's. However, this was how Stacy ignored his own abuse as a child. He brushed it under the rug and continued to build walls.

With kid gloves, slowly and gently, Stacy helped Isabelle to grow and blossom into the woman he saw every time he looked at her. What Isabelle didn't realize was, all along, she had taught Stacy what it felt like to fall in love. Being from vastly different worlds, they struggled to understand each other. Isabelle wondered if this relationship would work out, while Stacy was content with the way things were. He wasn't ready to move on to the next level in their relationship. Even a love like he's never had before couldn't help him tear down the walls he'd built. Will he ever be free, he wondered as he watched the road fade in his rearview mirror. He smiles at Isabelle and knows he must try to come to terms with his past or lose her forever.

ALSO BY K.C. POITRAS

You Taught Me What It Feels Like To Fall In Love

LETTER FROM THE AUTHOR

Dear Readers,

First, I'd like to thank each and every one of you that picked up my book, "Unseen," to read. This story was not an easy one to write. It tore at my heart to know there are many families that suffer through the same abuse as in this book. Just know, it is not ok to stand by and witness abuse of any kind. As adults, neighbors, friends or family, it is our obligation to protect innocent children. No child deserves mental, physical, or sexual abuse ever. Let me repeat that: No child deserves mental, physical, or sexual abuse ever.

Second, no human deserves mental, physical, or sexual abuse ever. There are many local, state and federal agency where help can be found. I have included national help lines and websites in hopes that if you are a victim, or if you are a person that knows a victim, that you reach out and seek help in guiding the way of that victim's future. There is also help for those that inflict abuse. You can be helped as well, look in the mirror, recognize the illness you harbor, and take action to make a change.

I hope this information is helpful, but it is my biggest hope that child abuse becomes less and less frequent. However, with the current state of the US and COVID, it's my belief it has become more and more frequent with lockdowns. Remember it takes a village to raise a child, be vigilant and proactive. Remember, a child acting out is most likely one that is seeking help of some kind. Take that moment and see if you can help.

Love to all.

KC Poitras

ACKNOWLEDGMENTS

This book is dedicated to my *person*, Eric. Without your tireless support in me and my writing, I wouldn't have made it this far, you've made my dreams come true. You are always ready to be my sounding board, my cheerleader, my provider of snacks, and my shoulder to cry on when things do not work out the way they are supposed to. You believe in me when I do not believe in myself and have given me more than you can possibly know. Without you this book, "Unseen," would have not been possible.

I would like to thank the following people for their help and support during the endeavor of my second book. Without them I could never have finished the book. So, thank you from the bottom of my heart for all you have done.

My Editor and Mentor, Colleen Voicework for her plentiful corrections and infinite patience. She's provided priceless advice during the entire process. Colleenvoicework.com.

Social media manager Deanna Martinez-Bey http://www. deannamartinezbey.com/ what a spectacular job she's done with marketing.

Responsible for my beautiful book cover is Oliviaprodesign. Thanks for taking my vision and making it a reality.

My Beta readers who always supported me and gave me their honest opinions, whether or not I was ready for them. Without your help, I may never have gotten this project to these final stages. Lorie Debo a long-time friend, Arlia a friend who I am lucky enough to have as a neighbor.

And of course, my daughter Eden for use of a photo.

I look forward to continued work with all of you. There are many more adventures to come and I am looking forward to sharing them with you!

CHILD ABUSE RESOURCES

CALL 1-800-4-A-CHILD (1-800-422-4453) then push 1 to talk to a hotline counselor. The Childhelp National Child Abuse Hotline is open 24 hours a day, 7 days a week. The hotline counselors work with translators who speak more than 200 languages to help callers who speak a language other than English. All calls are anonymous. (The hotline counselors don't know who you are, and you don't have to tell them.) https://www.childhelp.org/resources-kids/

Want to donate to the Childhelp National Child abuse organization? You can do so here: **https://give.childhelprelief.org/give/295966/#!/donation/checkout**

To report abuse on the state level, you can go here to find your state's information:

https://www.childwelfare.gov/organizations/?CWIGFunctionsaction=rols:main.dspList&rolType=Custom&RS_ID=%205

Or find your state below:

State toll-free numbers and websites for specific agencies designated to receive and investigate reports of suspected child abuse and neglect.

Alabama

Alabama

https://dhr.alabama.gov/child-protective-services/child-abuse-neglect-reporting/

Click on the website above for information on reporting or call Childhelp (800-422-4453) for assistance.

nadid: 10441

Alaska

Alaska

Toll-Free: (800) 478-4444

Email: HSS.DBH@Alaska.gov

http://dhss.alaska.gov/ocs/Pages/default.aspx

To report via email: ReportChildAbuse@alaska.gov

nadid: 10442

Arizona

Arizona

Toll-Free: (888) SOS-CHILD (888-767-2445)

https://dcs.az.gov/

Arizona's Online Reporting Service for Mandated Reporters via secure website in non-emergency cases:

https://dcs.az.gov/report-child-abuse

nadid: 10443

Arkansas

Arkansas

Toll-Free: (800) 482-5964

https://humanservices.arkansas.gov/

nadid: 10444

California

California

https://www.cdss.ca.gov/reporting/report-abuse/child-protective-services/report-child-abuse

Click on the website above for information on reporting or call Childhelp (800-422-4453) for assistance.

nadid: 10445

Colorado

Colorado

Phone: 1-844-264-5437

Phone: (303) 866-5700

https://www.colorado.gov/cdhs

Click on the website above for information on reporting or call Childhelp (800-422-4453) for assistance.

nadid: 10446

Connecticut

Connecticut

Toll-Free: (800) 842-2288

TDD: (800) 624-5518

https://portal.ct.gov/DCF

nadid: 10447

Delaware

Delaware

Toll-Free: (800) 292-9582

https://kids.delaware.gov/

Online reporting

https://kids.delaware.gov/family-services/child-abuse-and-neglect-reporting/

nadid: 10448

District of Columbia

District of Columbia
Local (toll): (202) 671-SAFE (202-671-7233)
https://cfsa.dc.gov/service/report-child-abuse-and-neglect
nadid: 10449

Florida

Florida
Toll-Free: (800) 96-ABUSE (800-962-2873)
https://www.myflfamilies.com/service-programs/abuse-hotline/
Online   Reporting   http://www.myflfamilies.com/service-programs/abuse-hotline
nadid: 10450

Georgia

Georgia
Phone: (404) 657-3433
https://dfcs.georgia.gov/services/child-abuse-neglect
Click on the website above for information on reporting or call Childhelp (800-422-4453) for assistance.
nadid: 10451

Guam

Guam
Phone: (671) 475-2672
Phone: (671) 475-2653
nadid: 29797

Hawaii

Hawaii
Local (toll): (808) 832-5300
http://humanservices.hawaii.gov/ssd/home/child-welfare-services/

nadid: 10452

Idaho

Idaho
Phone: (208) 334-5437
Toll-Free: (855) 552-KIDS (5437)
https://healthandwelfare.idaho.gov/Children/AbuseNeglect/
ChildProtectionContactPhoneNumbers/tabid/475/Default.aspx
nadid: 10453

Illinois

Illinois
Toll-Free: (800) 252-2873
Local (toll): (217) 524-2606
https://www2.illinois.gov/dcfs/safekids/reporting/
Pages/index.aspx
Mandated reporters may use the online child abuse reporting
system in non-emergency situations.
nadid: 10454

Indiana

Indiana
Toll-Free: (800) 800-5556
https://www.in.gov/dcs/
nadid: 10455

Iowa

Iowa
Toll-Free: (800) 362-2178
https://dhs.iowa.gov/home
nadid: 17506

Kansas

Kansas
Toll-Free: (800) 922-5330
http://www.dcf.ks.gov/Pages/Report-Abuse-or-Neglect.aspx
Online reporting for mandated reporters in non-emergency situations
http://www.dcf.ks.gov/services/PPS/Pages/
KIPS/KIPSWebIntake.aspx
nadid: 10457

Kentucky

Kentucky
Toll-Free: (877) 597-2331
https://prd.webapps.chfs.ky.gov/reportabuse/home.aspx
nadid: 17507

Louisiana

Louisiana
Toll-Free: (855) 452-5437
http://dss.louisiana.gov/page/109
Online reporting portal for mandated reporters in non-emergency situations
https://mr.dcfs.la.gov/c/MR_PortalApp.app
nadid: 10459

Maine

Maine
Toll-Free: (800) 452-1999
TTY: (800) 963-9490
https://www.maine.gov/dhhs/ocfs/hotlines.htm
nadid: 10460

Maryland

Maryland
http://dhr.maryland.gov/child-protective-services/reporting-

suspected-child-abuse-or-neglect/local-offices/

Click on the website above for information on reporting or call Childhelp (800-422-4453) for assistance.

nadid: 10461

Massachusetts

Massachusetts
Toll-Free: (800) 792-5200
https://www.mass.gov/child-abuse-and-neglect
nadid: 10462

Michigan

Michigan
Toll-Free: (855) 444-3911
Fax: (616) 977-1154
https://www.michigan.gov/mdhhs/0,5885,7-339-73971_7119--
-,00.html
Mandated Reporter online reporting system coming soon
nadid: 10463

Minnesota

Minnesota
https://mn.gov/dhs/report-abuse/
Click on the website above for information on reporting or call Childhelp (800-422-4453) for assistance.
nadid: 10464

Mississippi

Mississippi
Phone: (601) 432-4570
Toll-Free: (800) 222-8000
https://www.mdcps.ms.gov/report-child-abuse-neglect/
https://reportabuse.mdcps.ms.gov/
Reporting via online system or by downloading the MDCPS

Report Child Abuse mobile app
https://www.mdcps.ms.gov/report-child-abuse-neglect/
nadid: 10465

Missouri

Missouri

Toll-Free: (800) 392-3738

https://dss.mo.gov/cd/keeping-kids-safe/can.htm

Click on the website above for information on reporting or call Childhelp (800-422-4453) for assistance. Online reporting for mandated reporters in non-emergency situations:

https://dss.mo.gov/cd/keeping-kids-safe/can.htm
nadid: 10466

Montana

Montana

Toll-Free: (866) 820-5437

https://dphhs.mt.gov/cfsd/index
nadid: 17508

Nebraska

Nebraska

Phone: (402) 471-3121

Toll-Free: (800) 652-1999

http://dhhs.ne.gov/Pages/Child-Abuse.aspx
nadid: 17509

Nevada

Nevada

http://dcfs.nv.gov/Programs/CWS/CPS/CPS/

Click on the website above for information on reporting or call Childhelp (800-422-4453) for assistance.

nadid: 10469

New Hampshire
New Hampshire
Phone: (603) 271-6562
Toll-Free: (800) 894-5533
https://www.dhhs.nh.gov/dcyf/cps/stop.htm
nadid: 10470

New Jersey
New Jersey
Toll-Free: (877) 652-2873
TDD: (800) 835-5510
TTY: (800) 835-5510
https://www.nj.gov/dcf/reporting/hotline/
nadid: 17510

New Mexico
New Mexico
Toll-Free: (855) 333-7233
https://cyfd.org/(opens in new window)
nadid: 10472

New York
New York
Toll-Free: (800) 342-3720
TDD: (800) 369-2437
Local (toll): (518) 474-8740
https://ocfs.ny.gov/main/cps/Default.asp
nadid: 10473

North Carolina
North Carolina
https://www.ncdhhs.gov/
Click on the website above for information on reporting or call
Childhelp (800-422-4453) for assistance.

nadid: 28960

North Dakota
North Dakota
http://www.nd.gov/dhs/services/childfamily/cps/#reporting
Click on the website above for information on reporting or call Childhelp (800-422-4453) for assistance.
nadid: 10475

Ohio
Ohio
Toll-Free: (855) 642-4453
http://jfs.ohio.gov/ocf/reportchildabuseandneglect.stm
nadid: 17512

Oklahoma
Oklahoma
Toll-Free: (800) 522-3511
https://www.ok.gov/health/Family_Health/
Family_Support_and_Prevention_Service/
Oklahoma_Child_Abuse_Hotline/index.html
nadid: 10477

Oregon
Oregon
Toll-Free: (855) 503-SAFE (7233)
https://www.oregon.gov/dhs/children/child-abuse/Pages/
Reporting-Numbers.aspx
Click on the website above for information on reporting or call Childhelp (800-422-4453) for assistance.
nadid: 17513

Pennsylvania
Pennsylvania

Toll-Free: (800) 932-0313
TDD: (866) 872-1677
https://www.dhs.pa.gov/contact/Pages/Report-Abuse.aspx
Online reporting portal for mandated reporters in non-emergency situations
https://www.compass.state.pa.us/cwis/public/home
nadid: 17514

Puerto Rico

Puerto Rico
Toll-Free: (800) 981-8333
Local (toll): (787) 749-1333
nadid: 14201

Rhode Island

Rhode Island
Phone: (401) 528-3500
Toll-Free: (800) RI-CHILD (800-742-4453)
http://www.dcyf.ri.gov/child-protective-services/
nadid: 10480

South Carolina

South Carolina
Toll-Free: 1-888-227-3487
https://dss.sc.gov/abuseneglect/report-child-abuse-and-neglect/
Click on the website above for information on reporting or call Childhelp (800-422-4453) for assistance.
nadid: 17515

South Dakota

South Dakota
TTY: (877) 244-0864
https://dss.sd.gov/childprotection/

Click on the website above for information on reporting or call Childhelp (800-422-4453) for assistance.

nadid: 17516

Tennessee

Tennessee

Toll-Free: (877) 237-0004

https://www.tn.gov/dcs/program-areas/child-safety/reporting/child-abuse.html

Online reporting

https://apps.tn.gov/carat/

nadid: 17517

Texas

Texas

Toll-Free: (800) 252-5400

https://www.dfps.state.tx.us/Contact_Us/report_abuse.asp

Online reporting

https://www.txabusehotline.org/Login/Default.aspx

nadid: 17518

U.S. Virgin Islands

Virgin Islands

http://www.dhs.gov.vi/contact/index.html(opens in new window)

nadid: 24632

Utah

Utah

Phone: 1-855-323-3237

https://dcfs.utah.gov/

nadid: 13060

Vermont

Vermont
After hours: (800) 649-5285
https://dcf.vermont.gov/protection/reporting
nadid: 10486

Virginia

Virginia
Toll-Free: (800) 552-7096
Local (toll): (804) 786-8536
https://www.dss.virginia.gov/family/cps/index.cgi
nadid: 10487

Washington

Washington
Toll-Free: (866) END-HARM (866-363-4276)
Toll-Free: (800) 562-5624
TTY: (800) 624-6186
https://www.dcyf.wa.gov/safety/report-abuse
nadid: 10488

West Virginia

West Virginia
Toll-Free: (800) 352-6513
https://dhhr.wv.gov/bcf/Services/Pages/Centralized-Intake-for-Abuse-and-Neglect.aspx
nadid: 17519

Wisconsin

Wisconsin
https://dcf.wisconsin.gov/reportabuse
Click on the website above for information on reporting or call Childhelp (800-422-4453) for assistance.
nadid: 10490

Wyoming

Wyoming

https://www.wyomingcac.org/prevent-child-abuse/reporting-child-abuse

Click on the website above for information on reporting or call Childhelp (800-422-4453) for assistance.

nadid: 10491